# CONTENTS

# CALPHALON

# PERFORMANCE AIR FRY CONVECTION OVEN

# COOKBOOK FOR BEGINNERS

1000-DAY DELICIOUS AND AFFORDABLE RECIPE FOR AIR FRYING, CONVECTION BAKING, CONVECTION...BAKE, HEAT AND TOAST

THOMAS GILMORE

# INTRODUCTION

## How Does the Calphalon Air Fryer Oven Work?

Air fryer is an oven feature that works like a countertop air fryer. Inside an air fryer oven, super-heated air circulates around the food to provide crispy, golden results without all the oil that deep-frying requires. Air fryer ovens eliminate the need for another countertop appliance by putting the same technology right in your oven.

## The Benefits of The Calphalon Air Fryer Oven

During the last few years, these appliances are arguably the most respected and trendy thing that is happening in the kitchen. In comparison to other ways of frying, there are several benefits to use an air fryer.

### 1. The Calphalon Air Fryer Oven May Stimulate Weight Loss

Higher intakes of fried foods are closely related to a higher risk of obesity. It is because deep-fried foods happen to be rich in fat and calories. Swapping from deep-fried foods to air-fried foods and reducing the daily consumption of unsanitary oils will help to minimize weight loss.

### 2. The Calphalon Air fryer Oven May Be More Stable Than Deep Fryers

Heating a huge container full of scalding oil requires deep-frying foods. This could pose a danger to defense. There is no chance of wasting, splashing, or inadvertently hitting hot oil as air fryers get hot. People should carefully use frying machines and follow guidelines to ensure safety.

### 3. The Calphalon Air fryer Oven May Save Lots of Space

You could enjoy this advantage if you have a tiny kitchen, or live in a dorm room or communal housing. These systems are often the size of a coffee maker. They do not take up too much space on the fridge, and it is typically easy to store or pass about.

### 4. The Quality of Electricity

These fryers are more powerful than an oven, and they are not going to heat up your home.

# Using Tips for the Calphalon Air Fryer Oven

### 1. Use the Right Cookware

A perforated pan (sometimes called a perforated crisper tray) allows air to circulate under and around your food for even crisping. If you don't have one, you can use an oven-safe cooling rack. Line the bottom of your oven with aluminum foil or put a baking sheet under the rack below to catch any drips or crumbs.

### 2. Spread Out the Food

If you overload your pan to the point where food is piled up or touching, the exteriors won't brown as well, and it will steam instead of bake or air-fry. Instead, spread it in an even layer with plenty of room between each piece for air to circulate.

### 3. Cut Your Food Wisely

There's a reason why french fries are in long sticks — it's because this shape maximizes their surface, providing plenty of exterior for browning. Cut foods into long sticks or small, bite-sized pieces. If you are cooking something like tofu, try tearing it into pieces instead of slicing. The craggy shape will encourage the jagged edges to get crisp and brown.

### 4. Prepare Food Properly

The drier your food is before it goes into the oven, the better. Also, spraying it lightly with cooking spray or brushing or tossing with a neutral oil (like vegetable or grapeseed oil) will help encourage browning and crisping and will give a hint of that deep-fried taste we love.

### 5. Be Sure to Flip

Air fryer recipes usually recommend flipping the food halfway through cooking. This helps it cook and brown evenly. Don't omit this step in the instructions if you're using a convection or regular oven. After you flip, spritzing the other side with more cooking spray will also ensure both sides are equally crisp.

### 6. Know How to Adjust a Recipe

Air fryers cook hotter and faster than a conventional oven, so be aware that your recipe might take a few minutes longer. Start checking it for doneness at the time indicated in the recipe, and if it doesn't look browned enough, check every three minutes until it's golden brown and delicious!

In terms of temperature, air fryer recipes usually recommend a temperature of 20 to 25 degrees lower than you'd cook that type of food in a conventional oven, but the same holds true for convection ovens, so you can likely use the same temperature setting in an air fryer recipe for your convection oven. Cooking in a regular oven or toaster oven without a convection fan? Crank up the temperature by 25 degrees and make sure the oven is fully preheated before putting the food inside.

## Tips on Cleaning Your Calphalon Air Fryer Oven

Along with the racks, your oven interior, exterior, and trays also require regular cleaning if the appliance is used frequently. Here are a few oven cleaning tips that you might find helpful:

- Remove and soak panel knobs in water and dish soap; this allows for thorough cleaning of both, the panel and knobs
- Use the self-cleaning option if your oven has one
- Stubborn grime on interior walls of your oven can be loosened and removed by spraying with a warm solution of 3 part water to 1 part vinegar; wipe with a damp cloth thereafter
- Fill the tray with hot soapy water and scrub when the water cools down
- Clean the inner glass door with a layer of water and baking soda paste (leave to sit for 15 minutes); wipe with a soft, damp cloth to remove traces of the baking soda
- Clean the exteriors glass with vinegar and water, or an eco-friendly glass cleaning product
- Be extremely careful with oven cleaner on natural stone surfaces, it makes it very easy to damage
- Even after utilizing commercial products with instructions, there's still a chance to damage your oven. Be careful spraying oven cleaner on stainless steel surfaces.

# BREAKFAST

## Cinnamon Toast

Servings: 2
Cooking Time: 2 Minutes

**Ingredients:**

- 1 tablespoon brown sugar
- 2 teaspoons margarine, at room temperature
- ¼ teaspoon ground cinnamon
- 2 slices whole wheat or multigrain bread

**Directions:**

1. Combine the sugar, margarine, and cinnamon in a small bowl with a fork until well blended. Spread each bread slice with equal portions of the mixture.
2. TOAST once, or until the sugar is melted and the bread is browned to your preference.

## Apple Maple Pudding

Servings: 4
Cooking Time: 20 Minutes

**Ingredients:**

- Pudding mixture:
- 2 eggs
- ½ cup brown sugar
- 4 tablespoons maple syrup
- 3 tablespoons unbleached flour
- 1 teaspoon baking powder
- 1 teaspoon vanilla extract
- ¼ cup chopped raisins
- ¼ cup chopped walnuts
- 2 medium apples, peeled and chopped

**Directions:**

1. Preheat the toaster oven to 350° F.
2. Combine the pudding mixture ingredients in a medium bowl, beating the eggs, sugar, and maple syrup together first, then adding the flour, baking powder, and vanilla. Add the raisins, nuts, and apples and mix thoroughly. Pour into an oiled or nonstick 8½ × 8½ × 2-inch square baking (cake) pan.
3. BAKE for 20 minutes, or until a toothpick inserted in the center comes out clean.
4. BROIL for 5 minutes, or until the top is lightly browned.

# Danish Pecan Pastry

Servings: 9

Cooking Time: 35 Minutes

**Ingredients:**

- 1 (8-ounce) can refrigerated crescent roll dough
- 1 (8-ounce) package cream cheese, softened
- ½ cup packed dark brown sugar
- 1 large egg
- ½ teaspoon pure vanilla extract
- 1 tablespoon maple syrup
- ½ chopped pecans, toasted (see tip)
- GLAZE
- 1 cup confectioners' sugar
- 1 tablespoon whole milk
- 1 tablespoon maple syrup
- ¼ cup chopped pecans, toasted

**Directions:**

1. Preheat the toaster oven to 375 ºF. Grease an 8 x 8-inch square baking pan.
2. Place the crescent roll dough on a lightly floured surface. Pinch the perforations together. Cut the dough in half to form two squares. Press one half of the dough into the bottom of the prepared pan.
3. Beat the cream cheese, brown sugar, egg, vanilla, and maple syrup in a large bowl using a handheld mixer, at medium-high speed, until smooth. Stir in the pecans. Spread evenly over the dough in the baking pan. Top with the remaining dough. Bake for 25 to 35 minutes. Let the pastry cool slightly.
4. Meanwhile, make the glaze: Whisk the confectioners' sugar, milk, and maple syrup in a small bowl. Drizzle over the pastry. Sprinkle with the ¼ cup pecans. Refrigerate any leftovers.

# French Toast

Servings: 4

Cooking Time: 40 Minutes

**Ingredients:**

- 2 eggs
- 1 cup skim milk or low-fat soy milk
- 1 tablespoon honey
- Salt
- 4 slices multigrain bread
- Vegetable oil

**Directions:**

1. Whisk together the eggs, milk, honey, and salt to taste in a shallow bowl. Add a bread slice to the mixture and let it soak for one minute. Carefully turn it over and let the liquid saturate the other side. With a spatula, place the bread slice in an oiled 6½ × 6½ × 2-inch square (cake) pan.
2. BROIL for 5 minutes, then turn carefully with a spatula and broil for another 5 minutes, or until golden brown. Repeat the soaking and broiling procedure for the remaining slices.

# Paleo Spiced Zucchini Bread

Servings: 8

Cooking Time: 45 Minutes

**Ingredients:**

- Dry Ingredients
- 1½ cups almond flour
- 2 tablespoons coconut flour
- 1 teaspoon cinnamon
- ¼ teaspoon allspice
- ⅛ teaspoon ground cloves
- 1 teaspoon baking powder
- ½ teaspoon baking soda
- ¼ teaspoon salt
- 1 cup chopped walnuts
- Wet Ingredients
- ⅓ cup coconut sugar
- 1 teaspoon vanilla extract
- 3 large eggs
- 5 tablespoons olive oil
- 2 tablespoons applesauce
- 1 cup shredded zucchini, squeezed to remove excess moisture

**Directions:**

1. Stir together all the dry ingredients in a large bowl.
2. Whisk all the wet ingredients in a separate bowl.
3. Add the dry ingredients to the wet ingredients and stir to combine. Allow the batter to rest for 5 minutes. This allows the coconut flour to absorb the batter.
4. Preheat the toaster Oven to 350°F.
5. Grease the mini loaf pans with coconut oil spray. Divide the batter evenly between the pans.
6. Place the mini loaf pans on the wire rack, then insert the rack at mid position in the preheated oven.
7. Select the Bake function, adjust time to 45 minutes, and press Start/Pause.
8. Remove when a toothpick or cake tester inserted into the middle comes out clean.
9. Remove zucchini bread from the pans and place on a cooling rack for 15 minutes before slicing.

# Baked Eggs With Bacon-tomato Sauce

Servings: 1
Cooking Time: 12 Minutes

**Ingredients:**

- 1 teaspoon olive oil
- 2 tablespoons finely chopped onion
- 1 teaspoon chopped fresh oregano
- pinch crushed red pepper flakes
- 1 (14-ounce) can crushed or diced tomatoes
- salt and freshly ground black pepper
- 2 slices of bacon, chopped
- 2 large eggs
- ¼ cup grated Cheddar cheese
- fresh parsley, chopped

**Directions:**

1. Start by making the tomato sauce. Preheat a medium saucepan over medium heat on the stovetop. Add the olive oil and sauté the onion, oregano and pepper flakes for 5 minutes. Add the tomatoes and bring to a simmer. Season with salt and freshly ground black pepper and simmer for 10 minutes.
2. Meanwhile, preheat the toaster oven to 400°F and pour a little water into the bottom of the air fryer oven. (This will help prevent the grease that drips into the bottom drawer from burning and smoking.) Place the bacon in the air fryer oven and air-fry at 400°F for 5 minutes.
3. When the bacon is almost crispy, remove it to a paper-towel lined plate and rinse out the air fryer oven, draining away the bacon grease.
4. Transfer the tomato sauce to a shallow 7-inch pie dish. Crack the eggs on top of the sauce and scatter the cooked bacon back on top. Season with salt and freshly ground black pepper and transfer the pie dish into the air fryer oven. You can use an aluminum foil sling to help with this by taking a long piece of aluminum foil, folding it in half lengthwise twice until it is roughly 26-inches by 3-inches. Place this under the pie dish and hold the ends of the foil to move the pie dish in and out of the air fryer oven. Tuck the ends of the foil beside the pie dish while it cooks in the air fryer oven.
5. Air-fry at 400°F for 5 minutes, or until the eggs are almost cooked to your liking. Sprinkle cheese on top and air-fry for an additional 2 minutes. When the cheese has melted, remove the pie dish from the air fryer oven, sprinkle with a little chopped parsley and let the eggs cool for a few minutes – just enough time to toast some buttered bread in your air fryer oven!

## Hole In One

Servings: 1

Cooking Time: 7 Minutes

**Ingredients:**

- 1 slice bread
- 1 teaspoon soft butter
- 1 egg
- salt and pepper
- 1 tablespoon shredded Cheddar cheese
- 2 teaspoons diced ham

**Directions:**

1. Place a 6 x 6-inch baking dish inside air fryer oven and preheat fryer to 330°F.
2. Using a 2½-inch-diameter biscuit cutter, cut a hole in center of bread slice.
3. Spread softened butter on both sides of bread.
4. Lay bread slice in baking dish and crack egg into the hole. Sprinkle egg with salt and pepper to taste.
5. Air-fry for 5 minutes.
6. Turn toast over and top it with shredded cheese and diced ham.
7. Air-fry for 2 more minutes or until yolk is done to your liking.

## Brunch Burritos

Servings: 4

Cooking Time: 14 Minutes

**Ingredients:**

- Egg mixture:
- 4 medium eggs, lightly beaten
- 3 tablespoons finely chopped bell pepper
- 2 tablespoons finely chopped onion
- 4 strips lean turkey bacon, uncooked and cut into small ¼ × ¼-inch pieces
- 1 tablespoon chopped fresh cilantro
- ½ teaspoon ground cumin
- ½ teaspoon chili powder
- Salt and red pepper flakes to taste
- 4 6-inch flour tortillas
- 4 tablespoons salsa
- 4 tablespoons shredded part-skim, low-moisture mozzarella

**Directions:**

1. Combine the egg mixture ingredients in an oiled or nonstick 8½ × 8½ × 2-inch square baking (cake) pan.
2. TOAST twice, or until the mixture is firm and cooked.
3. Spoon the egg mixture in equal portions onto the center of each tortilla. Add 1 tablespoon salsa and 1 tablespoon mozzarella cheese to each. Roll each tortilla around the filling and lay, seam side down, in an oiled or nonstick 8½ × 8½ × 2-inch square baking (cake) pan.
4. BROIL for 8 minutes, or until lightly browned.

# Pecan-topped Baked Oatmeal

Servings: 6
Cooking Time: 45 Minutes

**Ingredients:**

- 2 tablespoons unsalted butter, plus additional for the pan
- 2 large eggs
- 3 cups whole milk
- ¼ cup packed dark brown sugar
- 1 teaspoon ground cinnamon
- 1 teaspoon pure vanilla extract
- ¼ teaspoon kosher salt
- 3 cups old-fashioned oats
- TOPPING
- ¼ cup packed dark brown sugar
- ½ cup chopped pecans
- Fresh blueberries (optional)
- Milk (optional)

**Directions:**

1. Lightly butter an 8 x 8-inch square baking pan.
2. Melt 2 tablespoons butter; set aside to cool slightly.
3. Whisk the eggs in a large bowl. Add the milk, brown sugar, cinnamon, vanilla, and salt and whisk to combine. Stir in the oats. Stir in the melted butter. Pour into the prepared pan. Cover and refrigerate overnight.
4. When ready to bake, preheat the toaster oven to 350°F. Gently stir the oat mixture in the baking pan.
5. Make the topping: Blend the brown sugar and pecans in a small bowl. Sprinkle the pecan mixture over the top of the oats. Bake, uncovered, for 40 to 45 minutes or until it is set and a knife inserted in the center comes out clean.
6. Sprinkle with fresh blueberries, if desired. Spoon into bowls and serve with milk to drizzle on top.

## Spicy Beef Fajitas

Servings: 4
Cooking Time: 40 Minutes

**Ingredients:**

- Mixture:
- 1 pound flank steak, cut into thin strips
- 2 inches long
- 1 bell pepper, seeded and cut into thin strips
- 2 tablespoons chopped onion
- 1 tablespoon chopped fresh cilantro
- ¼ teaspoon hot sauce
- 1 teaspoon garlic powder
- ½ teaspoon cumin
- 1 teaspoon chili powder
- Salt and freshly ground black pepper to taste
- 4 8-inch flour tortillas

**Directions:**

1. Combine all the mixture ingredients in an oiled or nonstick 8½ × 8½ × 2-inch square baking (cake) pan.
2. BROIL for 20 minutes, turning every 5 minutes, or until the pepper and onion are tender and the meat is beginning to brown. Remove from the oven and place equal portions of the mixture in the center of each tortilla. Roll the tortilla around the mixture and lay, seam side down, in a shallow baking pan.
3. BAKE at 350° F. for 20 minutes, or until the tortillas are lightly browned.

## Yogurt Bread

Servings: 2
Cooking Time: 40 Minutes

**Ingredients:**

- 3 cups unbleached flour
- 4 teaspoons baking powder
- 5 2 teaspoons sugar
- Salt to taste
- 1 cup plain nonfat yogurt
- ¼ cup vegetable oil
- 1 egg, beaten, to brush the top

**Directions:**

1. Preheat the toaster oven to 375° F.
2. Combine the flour, baking powder, sugar, and salt in a large bowl. Make a hole in the center and spoon in the yogurt and oil.
3. Stir the flour into the center. When the dough is well mixed, turn it out onto a lightly floured surface and knead for 8 minutes, until the dough is smooth and elastic. Place the dough in an oiled or nonstick regular-size 8½ × 4½ × 2¼-inch loaf pan. Brush the top with the beaten egg.
4. BAKE for 40 minutes, or until a toothpick inserted in the center comes out clean and the loaf is browned. Invert on a wire rack to cool.

# French Toast Casserole

Servings: 6
Cooking Time: 60 Minutes

**Ingredients:**

- 1 tablespoon unsalted butter, softened, plus 6 tablespoons unsalted butter, melted, divided
- ¾ cup packed (5¼ ounces) brown sugar
- 1 tablespoon ground cinnamon
- ½ teaspoon ground nutmeg
- ⅛ teaspoon table salt
- 18 slices potato sandwich bread, divided
- 2½ cups whole milk
- 6 large eggs
- ¼ cup sliced almonds, toasted
- Confectioners' sugar

**Directions:**

1. Adjust toaster oven rack to middle position and preheat the toaster oven to 350 degrees. Grease 13 by 9-inch baking dish with softened butter. Mix brown sugar, cinnamon, nutmeg, and salt together in bowl.
2. Sprinkle 3 tablespoons brown sugar mixture evenly over bottom of prepared dish. Place 6 bread slices (use bread heels here) in even layer in bottom of dish. Brush bread with 1½ tablespoons melted butter and sprinkle with 3 tablespoons sugar mixture.
3. Place 6 bread slices in single layer over first layer, brush with 1½ tablespoons melted butter, then sprinkle with 3 tablespoons sugar mixture. Place remaining 6 bread slices over previous layer and brush with 1½ tablespoons melted butter.
4. In separate bowl, whisk milk and eggs until well combined, then pour evenly over bread. Gently press down on layers with spatula to saturate bread. (Casserole can be covered and refrigerated for up to 12 hours.)
5. Sprinkle with almonds and remaining sugar mixture. Bake until casserole is slightly puffed and golden brown and bubbling around edges, 30 to 35 minutes, rotating dish halfway through baking. Transfer dish to wire rack, brush with remaining 1½ tablespoons melted butter, and let cool for 15 minutes. Sprinkle with confectioners' sugar and serve.

# Huevos Rancheros

Servings: 2

Cooking Time: 60 Minutes

**Ingredients:**

- 1 (28-ounce) can diced tomatoes
- 1½ teaspoons packed brown sugar
- 1½ teaspoons lime juice
- 1 small onion, chopped
- ¼ cup canned chopped green chiles
- 2 tablespoons extra-virgin olive oil
- 1½ tablespoons chili powder
- 2 garlic cloves, sliced thin
- ¼ teaspoon plus ⅛ teaspoon table salt, divided
- 2 ounces pepper Jack cheese, shredded (½ cup)
- 4 large eggs
- ⅛ teaspoon pepper
- ½ avocado, halved, pitted, and diced
- 2 tablespoons minced fresh cilantro
- 2 scallions, sliced thin
- 4 (6-inch) corn tortillas, warmed

**Directions:**

1. Adjust toaster oven rack to middle position and preheat the toaster oven to 450 degrees. Drain tomatoes in fine-mesh strainer set over bowl, pressing with rubber spatula to extract as much juice as possible. Combine ¾ cup drained tomato juice, sugar, and lime juice in bowl; set aside. Discard remaining drained juice.
2. Combine tomatoes, onion, chiles, oil, chili powder, garlic, and ¼ teaspoon salt in bowl, then spread mixture evenly on small rimmed baking sheet. Roast until charred in spots, 25 to 30 minutes, stirring and redistributing mixture into even layer halfway through roasting.
3. Remove sheet from oven. Carefully stir reserved tomato juice mixture into roasted vegetables, season with salt and pepper to taste, and spread into even layer. Sprinkle pepper Jack over top and, using back of spoon, make 4 evenly spaced indentations in cheese, each about 3 inches in diameter. Crack 1 egg into each hole and sprinkle with remaining ⅛ teaspoon salt and pepper.
4. Roast until whites are just beginning to set but still have some movement when sheet is shaken, 7 to 8 minutes for runny yolks or 9 to 10 minutes for soft but set yolks. Top with avocado, cilantro, and scallions. Serve immediately with tortillas.

# French Toast Sticks

Servings: 4
Cooking Time: 8 Minutes

**Ingredients:**

- 2 eggs
- ¼ cup half-and-half
- ½ teaspoon vanilla extract
- 6 slices wheat bread, cut into 1-inch strips
- 1 teaspoon ground cinnamon
- 2 tablespoons granulated sugar
- Maple syrup or pureed strawberries for serving

**Directions:**

1. In an 8-x-12-inch casserole dish, whisk together the eggs, half-and-half, and vanilla. Lay the strips of bread into the baking dish and flip around. Allow the bread to soak up the egg mixture for 10 minutes.
2. Meanwhile, in a small bowl, stir together the cinnamon and sugar.
3. Place the soaked bread strips into the air fryer oven, not touching one another. Spray with cooking spray and sprinkle the cinnamon and sugar mixture onto the bread sticks.
4. Air fry the French toast sticks at 370°F for 8 minutes. Cook in batches, as needed.
5. Serve with maple syrup or pureed strawberries.

## Western Frittata

Servings: 1
Cooking Time: 19 Minutes

**Ingredients:**

- ½ red or green bell pepper, cut into ½-inch chunks
- 1 teaspoon olive oil
- 3 eggs, beaten
- ¼ cup grated Cheddar cheese
- ¼ cup diced cooked ham
- salt and freshly ground black pepper, to taste
- 1 teaspoon butter
- 1 teaspoon chopped fresh parsley

**Directions:**

1. Preheat the toaster oven to 400°F.
2. Toss the peppers with the olive oil and air-fry for 6 minutes, redistribute the ingredients once or twice during the process.
3. While the vegetables are cooking, beat the eggs well in a bowl, stir in the Cheddar cheese and ham, and season with salt and freshly ground black pepper. Add the air-fried peppers to this bowl when they have finished cooking.
4. Place a 6- or 7-inch non-stick metal cake pan into the air fryer oven with the butter using an aluminum sling to lower the pan into the air fryer oven. (Fold a piece of aluminum foil into a strip about 2-inches wide by 24-inches long.) Air-fry for 1 minute at 380°F to melt the butter. Remove the cake pan and rotate the pan to distribute the butter and grease the pan. Pour the egg mixture into the cake pan and return the pan to the air fryer oven, using the aluminum sling.
5. Air-fry at 380°F for 12 minutes, or until the frittata has puffed up and is lightly browned. Let the frittata sit in the air fryer oven for 5 minutes to cool to an edible temperature and set up. Remove the cake pan from the air fryer oven, sprinkle with parsley and serve immediately.

## Breakfast Pita

Servings: 2
Cooking Time: 3 Minutes

**Ingredients:**

- 1 5-inch whole wheat pita loaf
- 1 teaspoon olive oil
- 1 egg, well beaten
- 2 tablespoons shredded low-fat mozzarella cheese
- Garlic powder
- Salt and freshly ground black pepper

**Directions:**

1. Cut a circle out of the top layer of one pita bread loaf and remove the disk-shaped layer, leaving the bottom intact. Brush the pita loaf with the olive oil. Carefully pour the beaten egg into the cavity. Sprinkle with cheese and season with garlic powder and salt and pepper to taste.
2. TOAST once on the oven rack, or until the egg is cooked thoroughly and the cheese is lightly browned.

## Baked Egg Cups

Servings: 2
Cooking Time: 25 Minutes

**Ingredients:**

- Nonstick cooking spray
- 2 slices white or wheat bread
- 1 ½ teaspoons unsalted butter, softened
- 2 thin slices ham, cut into strips about ½ inch wide
- 2 to 3 tablespoons shredded Swiss or cheddar cheese
- 2 large eggs
- Kosher salt and freshly ground black pepper
- 2 teaspoons whole milk or half-and-half
- Optional toppings: minced fresh flat-leaf (Italian) parsley, basil, tarragon, or other fresh herb, chopped tomatoes, chopped avocado, green onion (white and green parts, thinly sliced)

**Directions:**

1. Preheat the toaster oven to 350°F. Spray 2 (8-ounce) oven-safe ramekins with nonstick cooking spray.
2. Trim the crusts off the bread. (Discard the crusts or save for another use.) Lightly spread one side of each slice of bread with butter. Gently press the bread down into the ramekins, butter-side up, shaping to fit. Trim the ham slices so they fit the cup and arrange the strips of ham evenly over the bread. (The ham strips should not overhang the edges of the cup.) Spoon the cheese evenly over the ham. Add the egg to each cup and season with salt and pepper. Drizzle 1 teaspoon milk over the top of the egg yolk in each cup.
3. Bake, uncovered, for 20 to 25 minutes or until the yolk is lightly set. Remove from the oven and let stand for 2 to 3 minutes. (The residual heat will continue to cook the egg yolk.) Top, as desired, with any of the various topping choices.

## Cherries Jubilee

Servings: 4
Cooking Time: 10 Minutes

**Ingredients:**

- 1 15-ounce can cherries, pitted and drained, with 2 tablespoons juice reserved
- 1 tablespoon orange juice
- 1 tablespoon sugar
- 1 tablespoon cornstarch
- ¼ cup warmed Kirsch or Cognac
- Vanilla yogurt or fat-free half-and-half

**Directions:**

1. Combine the reserved juice, orange juice, sugar, and cornstarch in a shallow baking pan, blending well.
2. BROIL for 5 minutes, or until the juice clarifies and thickens slightly. Add the cherries and heat, broiling for 5 minutes more and stirring to blend. Remove from the oven and transfer to a flameproof serving dish.
3. Spoon the Kirsch over the cherries and ignite. Top with vanilla yogurt or drizzle with warm fat-free half-and-half and serve.

## Almond Cranberry Granola

Servings: 12

Cooking Time: 9 Minutes

**Ingredients:**

- 2 tablespoons sesame seeds
- ¼ cup chopped almonds
- ¼ cup sunflower seeds
- ½ cup unsweetened shredded coconut
- 2 tablespoons unsalted butter, melted or at least softened
- 2 tablespoons coconut oil
- ⅓ cup honey
- 2½ cups oats
- ¼ teaspoon sea salt
- ½ cup dried cranberries

**Directions:**

1. In a large mixing bowl, stir together the sesame seeds, almonds, sunflower seeds, coconut, butter, coconut oil, honey, oats, and salt.
2. Line the air fryer oven with parchment paper. Punch 8 to 10 holes into the parchment paper with a fork so air can circulate. Pour the granola mixture onto the parchment paper.
3. Air fry the granola at 350°F for 9 minutes, stirring every 3 minutes.
4. When cooking is complete, stir in the dried cranberries and allow the mixture to cool. Store in an airtight container up to 2 weeks or freeze for 6 months.

# LUNCH AND DINNER

## Sun-dried Tomato Pizza

Servings: 4
Cooking Time: 25 Minutes

**Ingredients:**

- Tomato mixture:
- 1 cup chopped sun-dried tomatoes
- 2 tablespoons tomato paste
- 2 tablespoons olive oil
- 2 tablespoons chopped onion
- 2 garlic cloves, minced
- 1 teaspoon dried oregano
- 1 teaspoon dried basil
- Salt and red pepper flakes to taste
- 1 9-inch ready-made pizza crust
- 1 5-ounce can mushrooms
- ¼ cup pitted and sliced black olives
- ½ cup shredded low-fat mozzarella cheese

**Directions:**

1. Combine the tomato mixture ingredients with ½ cup water in an 8½ × 8½ × 2-inch square baking (cake) pan.
2. BROIL for 8 minutes, or until the tomatoes are softened. Remove from the oven and cool for 5 minutes.
3. Process the mixture in a blender or food processor until well blended. Spread on the pizza crust and layer with the mushrooms, olives, and cheese.
4. BAKE at 400° F. for 25 minutes, or until the cheese is melted.

## Gardener's Rice

Servings: 4
Cooking Time: 40 Minutes

**Ingredients:**

- ½ cup rice
- 2 tablespoons finely chopped scallions
- 2 small zucchini, finely chopped
- 1 bell pepper, finely chopped
- 1 small tomato, finely chopped
- ¼ cup frozen peas
- ¼ cup frozen corn
- 1 teaspoon ground cumin
- ½ teaspoon dried oregano or
- 1 teaspoon chopped fresh oregano
- Salt and freshly ground black pepper to taste

**Directions:**

1. Preheat the toaster oven to 400° F.
2. Combine all the ingredients with ¼ cups water in a 1-quart 8½ × 8½ × 4-inch ovenproof baking dish, stirring well to blend. Adjust the seasonings to taste. Cover with aluminum foil.
3. BAKE, covered, for 30 minutes, or until the rice and vegetables are almost cooked. Remove from the oven, uncover, and let stand for 10 minutes to complete the cooking. Fluff once more and adjust the seasonings before serving.

## Kashaburgers

Servings: 4

Cooking Time: 50 Minutes

**Ingredients:**

- 1 cup kasha
- 2 tablespoons minced onion or scallions
- 1 tablespoon minced garlic
- ½ cup multigrain bread crumbs
- 1 egg
- ¼ teaspoon paprika
- ½ teaspoon chili powder
- ¼ teaspoon sesame oil
- 1 tablespoon vegetable oil
- Salt and freshly ground black pepper to taste

**Directions:**

1. Preheat the toaster oven to 400° F.
2. Combine 2 cups water and the kasha in a 1-quart 8½ × 8½ × 4-inch ovenproof baking dish.
3. BAKE, uncovered, for 30 minutes, or until the grains are cooked. Remove from the oven and add all the other ingredients, stirring to mix well. When the mixture is cooled, shape into 4 to 6 patties and place on a rack with a broiling pan underneath.
4. BROIL for 20 minutes, turn with a spatula, then broil for another 10 minutes, or until browned.

## Yeast Dough For Two Pizzas

Servings: 8

Cooking Time: 20 Minutes

**Ingredients:**

- ¼ cup tepid water
- 1 cup tepid skim milk
- ½ teaspoon sugar
- 1 1¼-ounce envelope dry yeast
- 2 cups unbleached flour
- 1 tablespoon olive oil

**Directions:**

1. Preheat the toaster oven to 400° F.
2. Combine the water, milk, and sugar in a bowl. Add the yeast and set aside for 3 to 5 minutes, or until the yeast is dissolved.
3. Stir in the flour gradually, adding just enough to form a ball of the dough.
4. KNEAD on a floured surface until the dough is satiny, and then put the dough in a bowl in a warm place with a damp towel over the top. In 1 hour or when the dough has doubled in bulk, punch it down and divide it in half. Flatten the dough and spread it out to the desired thickness on an oiled or nonstick 9¾-inch-diameter pie pan. Spread with Homemade Pizza Sauce (recipe follows) and add any desired toppings.
5. BAKE for 20 minutes, or until the topping ingredients are cooked and the cheese is melted.

## Pesto Pizza

Servings: 1
Cooking Time: 20 Minutes

**Ingredients:**

- Topping:
- ½ cup chopped fresh basil
- 1 tablespoon pine nuts (pignoli)
- 1 tablespoon olive oil
- 2 tablespoons shredded Parmesan cheese
- 1 garlic clove, minced
- ½ teaspoon dried oregano or 1 tablespoon chopped fresh oregano
- 1 plum tomato, chopped
- Salt and pepper to taste
- 1 9-inch ready-made pizza crust
- 2 tablespoons shredded low-fat mozzarella

**Directions:**

1. Preheat the toaster oven to 375° F.
2. Combine the topping ingredients in a small bowl.
3. Process the mixture in a blender or food processor until smooth. Spread the mixture on the pizza crust, then sprinkle with the mozzarella cheese. Place the pizza crust on the toaster oven rack.
4. BAKE for 20 minutes, or until the cheese is melted and the crust is brown.

## Connecticut Garden Chowder

Servings: 4
Cooking Time: 60 Minutes

**Ingredients:**

- Soup:
- ½ cup peeled and shredded potato
- ½ cup shredded carrot
- ½ cup shredded celery 2 plum tomatoes, chopped
- 1 small zucchini, shredded
- 2 bay leaves
- ¼ teaspoon sage
- 1 teaspoon garlic powder
- Salt and butcher's pepper to taste
- Chowder base:
- 2 tablespoons reduced-fat cream cheese, at room temperature
- ½ cup fat-free half-and-half
- 2 tablespoons unbleached flour
- 2 tablespoons chopped fresh parsley

**Directions:**

1. Preheat the toaster oven to 375° F.
2. Combine the soup ingredients in a 1-quart 8½ × 8½ × 4-inch ovenproof baking dish, mixing well. Adjust the seasonings to taste.
3. BAKE, covered, for 40 minutes, or until the vegetables are tender.
4. Whisk the chowder mixture ingredients together until smooth. Add the mixture to the cooked soup ingredients and stir well to blend.
5. BAKE, uncovered for 20 minutes, or until the stock is thickened. Ladle the soup into individual soup bowls and garnish with the parsley.

## Meat Lovers Pan Pizza

Servings: 9

Cooking Time: 15 Minutes

**Ingredients:**

- Dough
- ¾ cup plus 1½ tablespoons warm water, 100°-110°F
- 1¾ teaspoons instant yeast
- 2 cups all-purpose flour, plus more for dusting
- 1 teaspoon kosher salt
- 1 tablespoon extra virgin olive oil, plus more for drizzling
- Toppings
- 6 tablespoons pizza sauce
- 8 ounces shredded low-moisture mozzarella
- Pepperoni slices
- 8 ounces cooked Italian sausage
- Crushed red pepper, for sprinkling
- Dried oregano, for sprinkling
- Black pepper, for sprinkling

**Directions:**

1. Pour water into a large mixing bowl, then whisk in the yeast. Allow to bloom for 10 minutes.
2. Add the flour and salt and mix with your hands until no dry flour remains.
3. Cover the dough tightly with plastic wrap and allow to rest at room temperature for 15 hours.
4. Add the olive oil and form into a ball.
5. Drizzle extra-virgin olive oil generously on the food tray and use your hands to coat evenly.
6. Place the dough on the food tray and spread it out slightly toward the corners of the pan.
7. Drizzle some more extra-virgin olive oil on top and use your hands to evenly coat the top of the dough.
8. Cover the dough and allow it to rest for 90 minutes.
9. Spread the dough out further so that it covers the bottom of the pan, then pop any bubbles that formed in the dough.
10. Spread pizza sauce on the dough, followed by cheese, then pepperoni and sausage.
11. Sprinkle the pizza with crushed red pepper, dried oregano, and black pepper.
12. Preheat the toaster Oven to 450°F.
13. Insert the pizza at low position in the preheated oven.
14. Select the Pizza function, adjust time to 15 minutes, and press Start/Pause.
15. Remove when done and allow to rest for 5 minutes before cutting.
16. Cut the pizza into squares and serve.

## Rosemary Lentils

Servings: 2
Cooking Time: 35 Minutes

**Ingredients:**

- ¼ cup lentils
- 1 tablespoon mashed Roasted Garlic
- 1 rosemary sprig
- 1 bay leaf
- Salt and freshly ground black pepper
- 2 tablespoons low-fat buttermilk
- 2 tablespoons tomato sauce

**Directions:**

1. Preheat the toaster oven to 400° F.
2. Combine the lentils, 1¼ cups water, garlic, rosemary sprig, and bay leaf in a 1-quart 8½ × 8½ × 4-inch ovenproof baking dish, stirring to blend well. Add the salt and pepper to taste. Cover with aluminum foil.
3. BAKE, covered, for 35 minutes, or until the lentils are tender. Remove the rosemary sprig and bay leaf and stir in the buttermilk and tomato sauce. Serve immediately.

## Individual Baked Eggplant Parmesan

Servings: 5
Cooking Time: 55 Minutes

**Ingredients:**

- 1 medium eggplant, cut into 1/2-inch thick slices
- 1 1/2 teaspoons salt
- 1 cup Slow Cooker Marinara Sauce
- 1 package (8 oz.) fresh mozzarella, cut into 8 slices, divided
- 1 package (0.75 oz.) fresh basil, leaves only, divided
- 1/4 cup grated Parmesan cheese, divided

**Directions:**

1. Sprinkle eggplant with salt and place in a colander to drain for 1 hour.
2. Preheat the toaster oven to 375°F. Spray baking pan and 5 (4-inch) ramekins with nonstick cooking spray.
3. Rinse eggplant thoroughly with water to remove salt. Press each slice between paper towels to remove extra water and salt. Place on papertowels to dry. Arrange a single layer of eggplant slices in baking pan.
4. Bake 25 to 30 minutes or until eggplant is tender. Remove slices to cooking rack. Repeat baking remaining eggplant. Reduce oven temperature to 350°F.
5. In each ramekin, layer 1 slice eggplant, 1 tablespoon sauce, 1 slice mozzarella, 1 basil leaf, 1 additional tablespoon sauce and sprinkle with Parmesan cheese. Repeat layers ending with a sprinkle of Parmesan cheese.
6. Bake 20 to 25 minutes or until cheese is melted and eggplant layers are heated through.

## Baked Picnic Pinto Beans

Servings: 4
Cooking Time: 40 Minutes

**Ingredients:**

- 1 tomato, peeled and finely chopped
- 2 15-ounce cans pinto beans, drained
- 6 lean turkey bacon strips, cooked, drained, and crumbled
- 1 cup good-quality dark beer or ale
- 3 tablespoons finely chopped onion
- 1 tablespoon ketchup
- 2 tablespoons molasses
- 1 teaspoon Dijon mustard
- 1 teaspoon Worcestershire sauce
- 1 teaspoon garlic powder
- Salt and butcher's pepper to taste

**Directions:**

1. Preheat the toaster oven to 375° F.
2. Peel the tomato by immersing it in boiling water for 1 minute. Remove with tongs and when cool enough to handle, pull the skin away with a sharp paring knife. Chop and place in a 1-quart 8½ × 8½ × 4-inch ovenproof baking dish. Add all the other ingredients, stirring to mix well. Adjust the seasonings to taste. Cover with aluminum foil.
3. BAKE, covered, for 40 minutes.

## Kasha Loaf

Servings: 4
Cooking Time: 30 Minutes

**Ingredients:**

- 1 cup whole grain kasha
- 2 cups tomato sauce or 3 2 8-ounce cans tomato sauce (add a small amount of water to make 4 2 cups)
- 3 tablespoons minced onion or scallions
- 1 tablespoon minced garlic
- 1 cup multigrain bread crumbs
- 1 egg
- 1 teaspoon paprika
- 1 teaspoon chili powder
- 1 teaspoon sesame oil

**Directions:**

1. Preheat the toaster oven to 400° F.
2. Combine all the ingredients in a bowl and transfer to an oiled or nonstick regular-size 4½ × 8½ × 2/4-inch loaf pan.
3. BAKE, uncovered, for 30 minutes, or until lightly browned.

## Cornucopia Casserole

Servings: 4
Cooking Time: 45 Minutes

**Ingredients:**

- 1 celery stalk, chopped
- 2 tablespoons chopped Vidalia onion
- 3 ½ bell pepper, chopped
- 1 carrot, peeled and chopped
- 1 small zucchini, chopped
- ½ cup green beans, cut into 1-inch Pieces
- ½ cup frozen peas ½ cup frozen corn
- ½ cup frozen broccoli florets
- ½ cup frozen cauliflower florets
- 2 tablespoons vegetable oil
- 1 teaspoon ground cumin
- 1 teaspoon garlic powder
- ½ teaspoon paprika
- Salt and freshly ground black pepper to taste
- ½ cup finely chopped pecans
- 3 tablespoons grated Parmesan cheese

**Directions:**

1. Preheat the toaster oven to 400° F.
2. Combine all the ingredients, except the pecans and Parmesan cheese, in a 1-quart 8½ × 8½ × 4-inch ovenproof baking dish and adjust the seasonings to taste. Cover with aluminum foil.
3. BAKE, covered, for 35 minutes, or until the vegetables are tender. Uncover, stir to distribute the liquid, and adjust the seasonings again. Sprinkle the top with the pecans and Parmesan cheese.
4. BROIL for 10 minutes, or until the pecans are lightly browned.

## Moroccan Couscous

Servings: 4
Cooking Time: 22 Minutes

**Ingredients:**

- 1 cup couscous
- 2 tablespoons finely chopped scallion
- 2 tablespoons finely chopped bell pepper
- 1 plum tomato, finely chopped
- 2 tablespoons chopped pitted black olives
- 1 tablespoon olive oil
- ¼ teaspoon ground cumin
- ¼ teaspoon ground cinnamon
- ¼ teaspoon turmeric Pinch of cayenne
- Salt and freshly ground black pepper to taste

**Directions:**

1. Preheat the toaster oven to 400° F.
2. Combine all the ingredients with ¼ cups water in a 1-quart 8½ × 8½ × 4-inch ovenproof baking dish. Adjust the seasonings to taste. Cover with aluminum foil.
3. BAKE, covered, for 12 minutes. Remove from the heat and fluff with a fork. Cover again and let stand for 10 minutes. Fluff once more before serving.

# Maple Bacon

Servings: 6

Cooking Time: 16 Minutes

**Ingredients:**

- 12 slices bacon
- ½ cup packed dark brown sugar
- 2 tablespoons maple syrup
- 1 teaspoon Dijon mustard
- 2 tablespoons red or white wine

**Directions:**

1. Preheat the toaster oven to 350°F. Line a 12 x 12-inch baking pan with aluminum foil.
2. Place 6 bacon strips on the prepared pan, leaving space between the strips. Bake for 10 minutes or until the bacon is almost crisp. Carefully drain the bacon and return it to the pan.
3. Combine the brown sugar, maple syrup, mustard, and wine in a small bowl. Blend until smooth. Brush the glaze over the bacon. Bake for 8 minutes. Turn the bacon and brush with the glaze. Continue to bake for an additional 6 to 8 minutes, or until golden brown.
4. Repeat with the remaining bacon strips.

# Thai Chicken Pizza With Cauliflower Crust

Servings: 6

Cooking Time: 20 Minutes

**Ingredients:**

- Nonstick cooking spray
- ½ large head cauliflower (about 1 pound), cut into florets (3 ½ to 4 cups)
- 2 large eggs, lightly beaten
- ⅓ cup shredded mozzarella cheese
- 3 tablespoons shredded Parmesan cheese
- 2 teaspoons Italian seasoning
- ½ teaspoon garlic powder
- Kosher salt and freshly ground black pepper
- SAUCE
- ¼ cup creamy peanut butter
- 1 ½ tablespoons reduced-sodium soy sauce
- 1 ½ tablespoons fresh lime juice
- 1 tablespoon honey
- 1 tablespoon unseasoned rice vinegar
- ½ teaspoon chili garlic sauce
- TOPPINGS
- 1 cup chopped or shredded cooked chicken
- 1 carrot, shredded
- 2 green onions, white and green portions, thinly sliced
- 1 cup shredded Monterey Jack cheese

**Directions:**

1. Preheat the toaster oven to 425°F. Line a 12-inch pizza pan with parchment paper. Spray with nonstick cooking spray.
2. Place the cauliflower in the work bowl of a food processor. Pulse until finely chopped. (Work in batches, as necessary, so as not to overload the food processor.) Transfer the cauliflower rice to a large, microwave-safe bowl. Add 1 tablespoon water. Cover and microwave on High (100 percent) power for 3 minutes or until the cauliflower is tender. Uncover and let the cauliflower cool to room temperature.
3. Spoon the cauliflower into a clean kitchen towel and twist to drain the cauliflower well. Return the drained cauliflower to the bowl. Stir in the eggs, mozzarella, Parmesan, Italian seasoning, and garlic powder and season with salt and pepper. Stir well.
4. Spoon the cauliflower mixture onto the prepared pan. Gently spread or pat the mixture into an even circle, about 11 inches in diameter. Bake for 12 to 15 minutes or until the crust is set and beginning to brown.
5. Meanwhile, make the sauce: Stir the peanut butter, soy sauce, lime juice, honey, vinegar, and chili garlic sauce in a small bowl.
6. Remove the cauliflower crust from the toaster oven. Spread the peanut sauce over the crust. Top with the chicken, carrot, green onions, and Monterey Jack cheese. Bake for 5 minutes or until hot and the cheese is melted.

## Baked Parsleyed Cheese Grits

Servings: 4

Cooking Time: 30 Minutes

**Ingredients:**

- 4 strips lean uncooked turkey bacon, cut in half
- 1 cup grits
- 2 cups skim or low-fat soy milk
- 1 egg
- ½ cup shredded Parmesan cheese
- 1 tablespoon chopped fresh parsley
- ½ teaspoon garlic powder
- Salt and butcher's pepper to taste

**Directions:**

1. Preheat the toaster oven to 350° F.
2. Layer an 8½ × 8½ × 2-inch square baking (cake) pan with the bacon strips.
3. Combine the remaining ingredients in a medium bowl and pour the mixture over the strips.
4. BAKE, uncovered, for 30 minutes, or until the grits are cooked. Cut into squares with a spatula and serve.

## Chicken Marengo

Servings: 4

Cooking Time: 30 Minutes

**Ingredients:**

- Chicken mixture:
- 2 skinless, boneless chicken breast halves, cut into 1 × 1-inch pieces
- 6 large shrimp, peeled, deveined, and cut into 1 × 1-inch pieces
- 2 plum tomatoes, chopped
- 1 tablespoon olive oil
- ½ cup dry white wine
- 3 garlic cloves, chopped
- 6 fresh mushrooms, rinsed quickly, patted dry, and thinly sliced
- 1 teaspoon dried tarragon
- 1 tablespoon chopped fresh parsley
- Salt and freshly ground black pepper to taste
- 2 hard-boiled eggs, peeled and sliced
- ½ cup pitted and sliced black olives
- 2 tablespoons chopped fresh parsley

**Directions:**

1. Preheat the toaster oven to 375° F.
2. Combine the chicken mixture ingredients in a 1-quart 8½ × 8½ × 4-inch ovenproof baking dish and adjust the seasonings to taste. Cover with aluminum foil.
3. BAKE, covered, for 30 minutes, or until the chicken and shrimp are tender.
4. Garnish with slices of hard-boiled eggs, black olives, and parsley.

## Very Quick Pizza

Servings: 1
Cooking Time: 3 Minutes

**Ingredients:**

- 2 tablespoons salsa
- 1 6-inch whole wheat pita bread
- 2 tablespoons shredded part-skim, low-moisture mozzarella cheese

**Directions:**

1. Spread the salsa on the pita bread and sprinkle with the cheese.
2. TOAST once, or until the cheese is melted.

## Salad Couscous

Servings: 4
Cooking Time: 10 Minutes

**Ingredients:**

- 1 10-ounce package precooked couscous
- 2 tablespoons olive oil
- Salt and freshly ground black pepper
- ¼ cup chopped fresh tomatoes
- 2 tablespoons chopped fresh basil leaves
- 1 tablespoon sliced almonds
- ½ bell pepper, chopped
- 3 scallions, chopped
- 2 tablespoons lemon juice

**Directions:**

1. Preheat the toaster oven to 400° F.
2. Mix together the couscous, 2 cups water, and olive oil in a 1-quart 8½ × 8½ × 4-inch ovenproof baking dish. Add salt and pepper to taste. Cover with aluminum foil.
3. BAKE, covered, for 10 minutes, or until the couscous is cooked. Remove from the oven, fluff with a fork and, when cool, add the tomatoes, basil leaves, almonds, pepper, scallions, and lemon juice. Adjust the seasonings to taste. Chill before serving.

# SNACKS APPETIZERS AND SIDES

## Asparagus With Pistachio Dukkah

Servings: 3

Cooking Time: 8 Minutes

**Ingredients:**

- Pistachio Dukkah Ingredients
- 3 tablespoons coriander seeds
- 1 tablespoon cumin seeds
- ½ cup shelled pistachios
- ¼ cup sesame seeds
- 1 teaspoon salt
- ½ teaspoon pepper
- Asparagus Ingredients
- 1 bundle asparagus spears
- 1 tablespoon olive oil
- Salt & pepper, to taste

**Directions:**

1. Make the pistachio dukkah by placing the coriander and cumin seeds in a skillet over medium heat. Toast for 2 minutes, or until fragrant. Transfer spices to a spice grinder or mortar and pestle. Allow spices to cool completely, then grind.
2. Toast the pistachios in a skillet for 5 minutes, or until golden brown and fragrant. Transfer to a cutting board and chop finely. Add the sesame seeds to the same skillet and toast for 2 minutes, or until golden brown and
3. fragrant. Transfer the pistachios, sesame seeds, coriander, and cumin seeds to a bowl. Add salt and pepper, then stir to combine.
4. Select the Preheat function on the Cosori Smart Air Fryer Toaster Oven, adjust temperature to 430°F, and press Start/Pause.
5. Line the food tray with foil, then place the asparagus on the tray. Drizzle with olive oil and season with salt and pepper.
6. Insert food tray at top position in the preheated oven.
7. Select the Air Fry function, adjust time to 8 minutes, and press Start/Pause.
8. Remove when asparagus is tender. Place asparagus on a serving dish and sprinkle with pistachio dukkah.
9. Pistachio dukkah can be stored at room temperature in a sealed jar or container for up to 4 weeks.

## Smoked Gouda Bacon Macaroni And Cheese

Servings: 10-12
Cooking Time: 30 Minutes

**Ingredients:**

- 1 (4 oz.) French baguette, torn
- 6 slices cooked bacon, chopped
- 1/4 cup loosely packed parsley
- 2 Tablespoons butter, melted
- 1 package (16 oz.) corkscrew or elbow pasta
- 1/3 cup butter
- 1/4 cup flour
- 4 cups milk
- 1 package (8 oz.) extra sharp Cheddar cheese, shredded
- 1 package (8 oz.) smoked Gouda cheese, shredded
- 2 1/2 teaspoons Creole seasoning

**Directions:**

1. Preheat the toaster oven to 400°F.
2. Using S-blade with food processor running, drop bread, 1/2 of the bacon and parsley into food chute. Process until finely chopped. Gradually add melted butter; process until crumbs form. Set aside.
3. Cook pasta according to package directions for al dente. Drain and rinse with cold water. Set aside.
4. Melt 1/3 cup butter in Dutch oven over medium-high heat. Gradually add flour, whisking until smooth, about 1 minute. Slowly add milk, stirring 8 to 10 minutes until mixture is thickened and smooth. Remove from heat.
5. Stir in cheeses, remaining bacon and Creole seasoning until cheese is melted. Fold in pasta.
6. Pour mixture into 11x7-inch baking dish sprayed with nonstick cooking spray. Sprinkle with breadcrumb mixture.
7. Bake 25 to 30 minutes or until crumbs are browned and mixture is heated through.

## Sausage Cheese Pinwheels

Servings: 16
Cooking Time: 22 Minutes

**Ingredients:**

- 1 sheet frozen puff pastry, about 9 inches square, thawed (½ of a 17.3-ounce package)
- ½ pound bulk sausage
- ¾ cup shredded cheddar cheese

**Directions:**

1. Preheat the toaster oven to 400°F. Grease a 12 x 12-inch baking pan.
2. Unfold the puff pastry on a lightly floured surface and roll into a 10 x 12-inch rectangle. Carefully spread the sausage over the surface of the rectangle to within ½ inch of all four edges. Sprinkle the cheese evenly over the sausage. Starting with the long side, roll up tightly and press the edges to seal.
3. Using a serrated knife, slice the roll into ½-inch-thick pieces. You will get about 16 slices. Place the slices, cut side up, in the prepared baking pan. Bake for 18 to 22 minutes or until golden and the sausage is cooked through.
4. Serve warm or at room temperature.

## Crispy Tofu Bites

Servings: 4
Cooking Time: 20 Minutes

**Ingredients:**

- 1 pound Extra firm unflavored tofu
- Vegetable oil spray

**Directions:**

1. Wrap the piece of tofu in a triple layer of paper towels. Place it on a wooden cutting board and set a large pot on top of it to press out excess moisture. Set aside for 10 minutes.
2. Preheat the toaster oven to 400°F.
3. Remove the pot and unwrap the tofu. Cut it into 1-inch cubes. Place these in a bowl and coat them generously with vegetable oil spray. Toss gently, then spray generously again before tossing, until all are glistening.
4. Gently pour the tofu pieces into the air fryer oven, spread them into as close to one layer as possible, and air-fry for 20 minutes, using kitchen tongs to gently rearrange the pieces at the 7- and 14-minute marks, until light brown and crisp.
5. Gently pour the tofu pieces onto a wire rack. Cool for 5 minutes before serving warm.

## Crispy Spiced Chickpeas

Servings: 4
Cooking Time: 12 Minutes

**Ingredients:**

- 1 (15 ounce) can chickpeas, drained, rinsed, and patted dry
- 1 tablespoon olive oil
- ½ teaspoon cumin
- ¼ teaspoon paprika
- ½ teaspoon ground fennel seeds
- ⅛ teaspoon cayenne pepper

**Directions:**

1. Combine all ingredients in a large bowl and stir to combine.
2. Preheat the toaster oven to 430°F.
3. Place chickpeas on the food tray, then insert the tray at mid position in the preheated oven.
4. Select the Air Fry function, adjust time to 12 minutes, and press Start/Pause.
5. Remove when chickpeas are crispy and golden.

# Avocado Fries, Vegan

Servings: 4
Cooking Time: 10 Minutes

**Ingredients:**

- ¼ cup almond or coconut milk
- 1 tablespoon lime juice
- ⅛ teaspoon hot sauce
- 2 tablespoons flour
- ¾ cup panko breadcrumbs
- ¼ cup cornmeal
- ¼ teaspoon salt
- 1 large avocado
- oil for misting or cooking spray

**Directions:**

1. In a small bowl, whisk together the almond or coconut milk, lime juice, and hot sauce.
2. Place flour on a sheet of wax paper.
3. Mix panko, cornmeal, and salt and place on another sheet of wax paper.
4. Split avocado in half and remove pit. Peel or use a spoon to lift avocado halves out of the skin.
5. Cut avocado lengthwise into ½-inch slices. Dip each in flour, then milk mixture, then roll in panko mixture.
6. Mist with oil or cooking spray and air-fry at 390°F for 10 minutes, until crust is brown and crispy.

# Crab Rangoon Dip With Wonton Chips

Servings: 6

Cooking Time: 18 Minutes

**Ingredients:**

- Wonton Chips:
- 1 (12-ounce) package wonton wrappers
- vegetable oil
- sea salt
- Crab Rangoon Dip:
- 8 ounces cream cheese, softened
- ¾ cup sour cream
- 1 teaspoon Worcestershire sauce
- 1½ teaspoons soy sauce
- 1 teaspoon sesame oil
- ⅛ teaspoon ground cayenne pepper
- ¼ teaspoon salt
- freshly ground black pepper
- 8 ounces cooked crabmeat
- 1 cup grated white Cheddar cheese
- ⅓ cup chopped scallions
- paprika (for garnish)

**Directions:**

1. Cut the wonton wrappers in half diagonally to form triangles. Working in batches, lay the wonton triangles on a flat surface and brush or spray both sides with vegetable oil.
2. Preheat the toaster oven to 370°F.
3. Place about 10 to 12 wonton triangles in the air fryer oven, letting them overlap slightly. Air-fry for just 2 minutes. Transfer the wonton chips to a large bowl and season immediately with sea salt. (You'll hear the chips start to spin around in the air fryer oven when they are almost done.) Repeat with the rest of wontons (keeping those fishing hands at bay!).
4. To make the dip, combine the cream cheese, sour cream, Worcestershire sauce, soy sauce, sesame oil, cayenne pepper, salt, and freshly ground black pepper in a bowl. Mix well and then fold in the crabmeat, Cheddar cheese, and scallions.
5. Transfer the dip to a 7-inch ceramic baking pan or shallow casserole dish. Sprinkle paprika on top and cover the dish with aluminum foil. Lower the dish into the air fryer oven using a sling made of aluminum foil (fold a piece of aluminum foil into a strip about 2-inches wide by 24-inches long). Air-fry for 11 minutes. Remove the aluminum foil and air-fry for another 5 minutes to finish cooking and brown the top. Serve hot with the wonton chips.

## Chicken Shawarma Bites

Servings: 6
Cooking Time: 22 Minutes

**Ingredients:**

- 1½ pounds Boneless skinless chicken thighs, trimmed of any fat and cut into 1-inch pieces
- 1½ tablespoons Olive oil
- Up to 1½ tablespoons Minced garlic
- ½ teaspoon Table salt
- ¼ teaspoon Ground cardamom
- ¼ teaspoon Ground cinnamon
- ¼ teaspoon Ground cumin
- ¼ teaspoon Mild paprika
- Up to a ¼ teaspoon Grated nutmeg
- ¼ teaspoon Ground black pepper

**Directions:**

1. Preheat the toaster oven to 400°F.
2. Mix all the ingredients in a large bowl until the chicken is thoroughly and evenly coated in the oil and spices.
3. When the machine is at temperature, scrape the coated chicken pieces into the air fryer oven and spread them out into one layer as much as you can. Air-fry for 22 minutes, rotate at least three times during cooking to rearrange the pieces, until well browned and crisp.
4. Pour the chicken pieces onto a wire rack. Cool for 5 minutes before serving.

# Homemade Harissa

Servings: 20

Cooking Time: 20 Minutes

**Ingredients:**

- 2 red bell peppers, halved, cored, and seeded
- 1 teaspoon cumin seeds
- 1 teaspoon coriander seeds
- 4 tablespoons olive oil
- 1 cup onions, chopped
- 5 garlic cloves, minced
- 1 serrano chile, chopped (remove seeds to make less spicy)
- 1 lemon, juiced
- ½ teaspoon salt

**Directions:**

1. Select the Preheat function on the Cosori Smart Air Fryer Toaster Oven, adjust temperature to 450°F, and press Start/Pause.
2. Line the food tray with foil and place the bell pepper halves on the tray.
3. Insert the food tray at mid position in the preheated oven.
4. Select the Roast function, adjust time to 20 minutes, and press Start/Pause.
5. Remove when bell peppers are charred. Immediately place bell peppers into a bowl and cover tightly with plastic wrap. Allow peppers to steam for 15 minutes. Remove plastic wrap, peel the skin off the peppers, and place into a food processor.
6. Place cumin and coriander seeds in a dry skillet. Toast over medium heat for 4-5 minutes or until fragrant.
7. Place seeds into a mortar and pestle or spice grinder and grind to a powder. Place into the food processor.
8. Heat olive oil in a pan over medium heat. Add the onion and garlic and saute for 10 minutes or until they begin to soften and caramelize. Place into the food processor.
9. Place the remaining ingredients into the food processor and blend until smooth. Taste and add additional lemon juice, salt, or olive oil if needed.
10. Store harissa in a sealed jar for up to 2 weeks.

## Roasted Brussels Sprouts

Servings: 2
Cooking Time: 30 Minutes

**Ingredients:**

- 12 ounces brussels sprouts, trimmed and halved
- 4 teaspoons water
- 1 tablespoon extra-virgin olive oil
- ⅛ teaspoon table salt
- Pinch pepper
- Lemon wedges

**Directions:**

1. Adjust toaster oven rack to middle position and preheat the toaster oven to 450 degrees. Toss brussels sprouts, water, oil, salt, and pepper together on small rimmed baking sheet, then arrange cut side down on sheet in even layer.
2. Cover sheet tightly with aluminum foil and roast for 10 minutes. Remove foil and continue to roast until sprouts are browned and tender, 10 to 15 minutes. Season with salt and pepper. Serve with lemon wedges.

## Fried Green Tomatoes

Servings: 4
Cooking Time: 15 Minutes

**Ingredients:**

- 2 eggs
- ¼ cup buttermilk
- ½ cup cornmeal
- ½ cup breadcrumbs
- ¼ teaspoon salt
- 1½ pounds firm green tomatoes, cut in ¼-inch slices
- oil for misting or cooking spray
- Horseradish Drizzle
- ¼ cup mayonnaise
- ¼ cup sour cream
- 2 teaspoons prepared horseradish
- ½ teaspoon Worcestershire sauce
- ½ teaspoon lemon juice
- ⅛ teaspoon black pepper

**Directions:**

1. Mix all ingredients for Horseradish Drizzle together and chill while you prepare the green tomatoes.
2. Preheat the toaster oven to 390°F.
3. Beat the eggs and buttermilk together in a shallow bowl.
4. Mix cornmeal, breadcrumbs, and salt together in a plate or shallow dish.
5. Dip 4 tomato slices in the egg mixture, then roll in the breadcrumb mixture.
6. Mist one side with oil and place in air fryer oven, oil-side down, in a single layer.
7. Mist the top with oil.
8. Air-fry for 15 minutes, turning once, until brown and crispy.
9. Repeat steps 5 through 8 to cook remaining tomatoes.
10. Drizzle horseradish sauce over tomatoes just before serving.

## Cheese Straws

Servings: 8

Cooking Time: 7 Minutes

**Ingredients:**

- For dusting All-purpose flour
- Two quarters of one thawed sheet (that is, a half of the sheet cut into two even pieces; wrap and refreeze the remainder) A 17.25-ounce box frozen puff pastry
- 1 Large egg(s)
- 2 tablespoons Water
- ¼ cup (about ¾ ounce) Finely grated Parmesan cheese
- up to 1 teaspoon Ground black pepper

**Directions:**

1. Preheat the toaster oven to 400°F.
2. Dust a clean, dry work surface with flour. Set one of the pieces of puff pastry on top, dust the pastry lightly with flour, and roll with a rolling pin to a 6-inch square.
3. Whisk the egg(s) and water in a small or medium bowl until uniform. Brush the pastry square(s) generously with this mixture. Sprinkle each square with 2 tablespoons grated cheese and up to ½ teaspoon ground black pepper.
4. Cut each square into 4 even strips. Grasp each end of 1 strip with clean, dry hands; twist it into a cheese straw. Place the twisted straws on a baking sheet.
5. Lay as many straws as will fit in the air-fryer oven—as a general rule, 4 of them in a small machine, 5 in a medium model, or 6 in a large. There should be space for air to circulate around the straws. Set the baking sheet with any remaining straws in the fridge.
6. Air-fry undisturbed for 7 minutes, or until puffed and crisp. Use tongs to transfer the cheese straws to a wire rack, then make subsequent batches in the same way (keeping the baking sheet with the remaining straws in the fridge as each batch cooks). Serve warm.

## Bagel Chips

Servings: 2

Cooking Time: 4 Minutes

**Ingredients:**

- Sweet
- 1 large plain bagel
- 2 teaspoons sugar
- 1 teaspoon ground cinnamon
- butter-flavored cooking spray
- Savory
- 1 large plain bagel
- 1 teaspoon Italian seasoning
- ½ teaspoon garlic powder
- oil for misting or cooking spray

**Directions:**

1. Preheat the toaster oven to 390°F.
2. Cut bagel into ¼-inch slices or thinner.
3. Mix the seasonings together.
4. Spread out the slices, mist with oil or cooking spray, and sprinkle with half of the seasonings.
5. Turn over and repeat to coat the other side with oil or cooking spray and seasonings.
6. Place in air fryer oven and air-fry for 2 minutes. Stir a little and continue cooking for 2 minutes or until toasty brown and crispy.

## Creamy Crab Dip

Servings: 4

Cooking Time: 20 Minutes

**Ingredients:**

- 6 ounces cream cheese, room temperature
- ½ cup sour cream
- ½ cup grated Parmesan cheese
- ½ cup shredded cheddar cheese
- Juice of ½ lemon
- ½ teaspoon garlic powder
- Dash hot sauce
- 1 (6-ounce) can crab meat, drained
- Sea salt, for seasoning
- Freshly ground black pepper, for seasoning
- Baguette, cut into ¼-inch-wide rounds, for serving

**Directions:**

1. Place the rack on position 1 and preheat the toaster oven on BAKE to 400°F for 5 minutes.
2. In a medium bowl, stir the cream cheese, sour cream, Parmesan, cheddar, lemon juice, garlic powder, and hot sauce until well blended.
3. Fold in the crab and season with salt and pepper.
4. Spoon the dip into a shallow heatproof 4-cup bowl.
5. Bake for 20 minutes until golden and bubbling.
6. Serve with baguette slices.

## Baked Asparagus Fries

Servings: 2-3
Cooking Time: 14 Minutes

**Ingredients:**

- 1 1/2 cups mayonnaise
- 3/4 cup grated Parmesan cheese
- 2 cloves garlic, minced
- 1 tablespoon dried parsley
- 1 tablespoon Italian seasoning
- 1 teaspoon salt
- 1/2 teaspoon coarse black pepper
- 1/2 pound thick asparagus, trimmed
- 1 cup panko crumbs

**Directions:**

1. Heat the oven to 425°F.
2. In a small bowl, combine mayonnaise, Parmesan cheese, garlic, parsley, Italian seasoning, salt and black pepper.
3. Brush asparagus with 3 tablespoons mayonnaise mixture and roll in crumbs. Place asparagus on the baking pan.
4. Bake 12 to 14 minutes or until lightly browned and asparagus are cooked.
5. Serve asparagus with the remaining mayonnaise mixture.

## Bacon Corn Muffins

Servings: 6
Cooking Time: 17 Minutes

**Ingredients:**

- 1 1/4 cups self rising cornmeal mix
- 3/4 cup buttermilk
- 1/3 cup chopped cooked bacon
- 1/4 cup butter, melted
- 1 large egg, slightly beaten

**Directions:**

1. Preheat toaster oven to 425°F on CONVECTION setting.
2. Stir cornmeal mix, buttermilk, bacon, butter and egg until blended.
3. Spoon batter into lightly greased muffin pan, filling 3/4 full.
4. Bake 15 to 17 minutes until toothpick inserted in center comes out clean.
5. Cool 10 minutes on wire rack; remove.

# Roasted Pumpkin Seeds

Servings: 2-4

Cooking Time: 50 Minutes

**Ingredients:**

- 1 medium pumpkin
- 1 tablespoon vegetable oil
- Salt

**Directions:**

1. Preheat the toaster oven to 300°F. Line a baking sheet with parchment paper. Set aside.
2. Cut the top from the pumpkin. Using a large spoon, scrape out the pulp and seeds from the pumpkin and place in a colander or strainer.
3. Separate the pulp and strings from seeds. Rinse seeds and pat dry with paper towels.
4. Spread the seeds on the prepared baking sheet.
5. Bake until the seeds are dry, about 30 minutes.
6. In a small bowl, toss seeds with oil and salt. Bake until seeds are toasted, an additional 15 to 20 minutes.

# Quick And Easy Nachos

Servings: 2
Cooking Time: 30 Minutes

**Ingredients:**

- 2 tomatoes, cored and chopped
- ¼ cup finely chopped red onion
- 1 tablespoon lime juice, plus lime wedges for serving
- 1 garlic clove, minced
- 6 ounces tortilla chips
- ½ cup refried beans
- 8 ounces cheddar cheese, shredded (2 cups)
- 2 scallions, sliced thin
- 1 jalapeño chile, stemmed, seeded, and sliced thin
- ¼ cup sour cream

**Directions:**

1. Combine tomatoes, onion, lime juice, and garlic in bowl and season with salt and pepper to taste; set salsa aside until ready to serve.
2. Adjust toaster oven rack to lowest position and preheat the toaster oven to 400 degrees. Spread half of chips in even layer in 8-inch square baking dish or pan. Dollop ¼ cup refried beans in 1 tablespoon-size portions over chips, then sprinkle evenly with 1 cup cheddar. Repeat with remaining chips, ¼ cup refried beans, and 1 cup cheddar.
3. Bake nachos until cheese is melted, 7 to 12 minutes. Remove nachos from toaster oven, let cool for 2 minutes, then sprinkle with scallions and jalapeño. Along edge of nachos, drop scoops of salsa and sour cream. Serve immediately with lime wedges.

# Parmesan Crisps

Servings: 6
Cooking Time: 7 Minutes

**Ingredients:**

- 6 tablespoons shredded Parmesan cheese

**Directions:**

1. Preheat the toaster oven to 350°F on BAKE for 10 minutes.
2. Line the baking tray with a silicone mat or parchment paper.
3. Place the Parmesan by tablespoons about 2 inches apart on the tray, spreading the cheese out in an even layer about 2½ inches in diameter.
4. Place the try in position 2 and bake for 7 minutes until the edges are browned, and the cheese is no longer bubbling.
5. Remove from the oven and allow to cool on the rack for 10 minutes before serving.

# FISH AND SEAFOOD

## Pecan-crusted Tilapia

Servings: 4
Cooking Time: 8 Minutes

**Ingredients:**

- 1 pound skinless, boneless tilapia filets
- ¼ cup butter, melted
- 1 teaspoon minced fresh or dried rosemary
- 1 cup finely chopped pecans
- 1 teaspoon sea salt
- ¼ teaspoon paprika
- 2 tablespoons chopped parsley
- 1 lemon, cut into wedges

**Directions:**

1. Pat the tilapia filets dry with paper towels.
2. Pour the melted butter over the filets and flip the filets to coat them completely.
3. In a medium bowl, mix together the rosemary, pecans, salt, and paprika.
4. Preheat the toaster oven to 350°F.
5. Place the tilapia filets into the air fryer oven and top with the pecan coating. Air-fry for 6 to 8 minutes. The fish should be firm to the touch and flake easily when fully cooked.
6. Remove the fish from the air fryer oven. Top the fish with chopped parsley and serve with lemon wedges.

## Baked Parsley Mussels With Zucchini

Servings: 6
Cooking Time: 40 Minutes

**Ingredients:**

- 2 pounds (approximately 40) mussels, cooked, shells discarded
- 4 small zucchini squash, scrubbed, halved, and cut lengthwise into ½-inch-wide strips
- ½ cup dry white wine
- 1 tablespoon chopped fresh oregano or 1 teaspoon dried oregano
- 2 garlic cloves, minced
- ¼ cup chopped fresh Italian parsley
- 2 tablespoons olive oil
- Freshly ground black pepper to taste
- ¼ cup grated low-fat Parmesan cheese

**Directions:**

1. Preheat the toaster oven to 350° F.
2. Combine all the ingredients except the Parmesan cheese in a 1-quart 8½ × 8½ × 4-inch ovenproof baking dish, mixing well. Adjust the seasonings to taste and cover with aluminum foil.
3. BAKE for 35 minutes, or until the zucchini is tender. Uncover and sprinkle with Parmesan cheese.
4. BROIL for 5 minutes, or until the cheese is melted and the top is lightly browned.

## Capered Crab Cakes

Servings: 6

Cooking Time: 30 Minutes

**Ingredients:**

- 1 pound fresh lump crabmeat, drained and chopped, or 3 5-ounce cans good-quality lump crabmeat
- 1 cup bread crumbs
- ½ cup plain nonfat yogurt
- 1 tablespoon olive oil
- 2 tablespoons capers
- 1 tablespoon garlic powder
- 1 teaspoon hot sauce
- 1 egg, beaten
- 1 tablespoon Worcestershire sauce
- Salt and freshly ground black pepper to taste

**Directions:**

1. Preheat the toaster oven to 350° F.
2. Combine all the ingredients in a bowl. Shape the mixture into patties approximately 2½ inches wide, adding more bread crumbs if the mixture is too wet and sticky and more yogurt if the mixture is too dry and crumbly. Place the patties in an 8½ × 8½ × 2-inch oiled or nonstick square (cake) pan.
3. BAKE, uncovered, for 25 minutes.
4. BROIL for 5 minutes, until golden brown.

## Snapper With Capers And Olives

Servings: 2

Cooking Time: 10 Minutes

**Ingredients:**

- 2 tablespoons capers
- ¼ cup pitted and sliced black olives
- 2 tablespoons olive oil
- ½ teaspoon dried oregano
- Salt and freshly ground black pepper to taste
- 2 6-ounce red snapper fillets
- 1 tomato, cut into wedges

**Directions:**

1. Combine the capers, olives, olive oil, and seasonings in a bowl.
2. Place the fillets in an oiled or nonstick 8½ × 8½ × 2-inch square baking (cake) pan and spoon the caper mixture over them.
3. BROIL for 10 minutes, or until the fish flakes easily with a fork. Serve with the tomato wedges.

# Coconut Jerk Shrimp

Servings: 3

Cooking Time: 8 Minutes

**Ingredients:**

- 1 Large egg white(s)
- 1 teaspoon Purchased or homemade jerk dried seasoning blend
- ¾ cup Plain panko bread crumbs (gluten-free, if a concern)
- ¾ cup Unsweetened shredded coconut
- 12 Large shrimp (20–25 per pound), peeled and deveined
- Coconut oil spray

**Directions:**

1. Preheat the toaster oven to 375°F .
2. Whisk the egg white(s) and seasoning blend in a bowl until foamy. Add the shrimp and toss well to coat evenly.
3. Mix the bread crumbs and coconut on a dinner plate until well combined. Use kitchen tongs to pick up a shrimp, letting the excess egg white mixture slip back into the rest. Set the shrimp in the bread-crumb mixture. Turn several times to coat evenly and thoroughly. Set on a cutting board and continue coating the remainder of the shrimp.
4. Lightly coat all the shrimp on both sides with the coconut oil spray. Set them in the air fryer oven in one layer with as much space between them as possible. (You can even stand some up along the air fryer oven's wall in some models.) Air-fry undisturbed for 6 minutes, or until the coating is lightly browned. If the air fryer oven is at 360°F, you may need to add 2 minutes to the cooking time.
5. Use clean kitchen tongs to transfer the shrimp to a wire rack. Cool for only a minute or two before serving.

# Coconut-shrimp Po' Boys

Servings: 4

Cooking Time: 5 Minutes

**Ingredients:**

- ½ cup cornstarch
- 2 eggs
- 2 tablespoons milk
- ¾ cup shredded coconut
- ½ cup panko breadcrumbs
- 1 pound (31–35 count) shrimp, peeled and deveined
- Old Bay Seasoning
- oil for misting or cooking spray
- 2 large hoagie rolls
- honey mustard or light mayonnaise
- 1½ cups shredded lettuce
- 1 large tomato, thinly sliced

**Directions:**

1. Place cornstarch in a shallow dish or plate.
2. In another shallow dish, beat together eggs and milk.
3. In a third dish mix the coconut and panko crumbs.
4. Sprinkle shrimp with Old Bay Seasoning to taste.
5. Dip shrimp in cornstarch to coat lightly, dip in egg mixture, shake off excess, and roll in coconut mixture to coat well.
6. Spray both sides of coated shrimp with oil or cooking spray.
7. Cook half the shrimp in a single layer at 390°F for 5 minutes.
8. Repeat to cook remaining shrimp.
9. To Assemble
10. Split each hoagie lengthwise, leaving one long edge intact.
11. Place in air fryer oven and air-fry at 390°F for 1 to 2 minutes or until heated through.
12. Remove buns, break apart, and place on 4 plates, cut side up.
13. Spread with honey mustard and/or mayonnaise.
14. Top with shredded lettuce, tomato slices, and coconut shrimp.

# Crunchy And Buttery Cod With Ritz® Cracker Crust

Servings: 2

Cooking Time: 10 Minutes

**Ingredients:**

- 4 tablespoons butter, melted
- 8 to 10 RITZ® crackers, crushed into crumbs
- 2 (6-ounce) cod fillets
- salt and freshly ground black pepper
- 1 lemon

**Directions:**

1. Preheat the toaster oven to 380°F.
2. Melt the butter in a small saucepan on the stovetop or in a microwavable dish in the microwave, and then transfer the butter to a shallow dish. Place the crushed RITZ® crackers into a second shallow dish.
3. Season the fish fillets with salt and freshly ground black pepper. Dip them into the butter and then coat both sides with the RITZ® crackers.
4. Place the fish into the air fryer oven and air-fry at 380°F for 10 minutes, flipping the fish over halfway through the cooking time.
5. Serve with a wedge of lemon to squeeze over the top.

## Crab Cakes

Servings: 4
Cooking Time: 9 Minutes

**Ingredients:**

- 1 pound lump crab meat, checked for shells
- ⅓ cup breadcrumbs
- ¼ cup finely chopped onions
- ¼ cup finely chopped red bell peppers
- ¼ cup finely chopped parsley
- ¼ teaspoon sea salt
- 2 eggs, whisked
- ¾ cup mayonnaise, divided
- ¼ cup sour cream
- 1 lemon, divided
- ¼ cup sweet pickle relish
- 1 tablespoon prepared mustard

**Directions:**

1. In a large bowl, mix together the crab meat, breadcrumbs, onions, bell peppers, parsley, sea salt, eggs, and ¼ cup of the mayonnaise.
2. Preheat the toaster oven to 380°F.
3. Form 8 patties with the crab cake mixture. Line the air fryer oven with parchment paper and place the crab cakes on the parchment paper. Spray with cooking spray. Air-fry for 4 minutes, turn over the crab cakes, spray with cooking spray, and air-fry for an additional 3 to 5 minutes, or until golden brown and the edges are crispy. Cook in batches as needed.
4. Meanwhile, make the sauce. In a small bowl, mix together the remaining ½ cup of mayonnaise, the sour cream, the juice from ½ of the lemon, the pickle relish, and the mustard.
5. Place the cooked crab cakes on a serving platter and serve with the remaining ½ lemon cut into wedges and the dipping sauce.

## Fish Sticks For Kids

Servings: 8
Cooking Time: 6 Minutes

**Ingredients:**

- 8 ounces fish fillets (pollock or cod)
- salt (optional)
- ½ cup plain breadcrumbs
- oil for misting or cooking spray

**Directions:**

1. Cut fish fillets into "fingers" about ½ x 3 inches. Sprinkle with salt to taste, if desired.
2. Roll fish in breadcrumbs. Spray all sides with oil or cooking spray.
3. Place in air fryer oven in single layer and air-fry at 390°F for 6 minutes, until golden brown and crispy.

## Shrimp

Servings: 4

Cooking Time: 8 Minutes

**Ingredients:**

- 1 pound (26–30 count) shrimp, peeled, deveined, and butterflied (last tail section of shell intact)
- Marinade
- 1 5-ounce can evaporated milk
- 2 eggs, beaten
- 2 tablespoons white vinegar
- 1 tablespoon baking powder
- Coating
- 1 cup crushed panko breadcrumbs
- ½ teaspoon paprika
- ½ teaspoon Old Bay Seasoning
- ¼ teaspoon garlic powder
- oil for misting or cooking spray

**Directions:**

1. Stir together all marinade ingredients until well mixed. Add shrimp and stir to coat. Refrigerate for 1 hour.
2. When ready to cook, preheat the toaster oven to 390°F.
3. Combine coating ingredients in shallow dish.
4. Remove shrimp from marinade, roll in crumb mixture, and spray with olive oil or cooking spray.
5. Cooking in two batches, place shrimp in air fryer oven in single layer, close but not overlapping. Air-fry at 390°F for 8 minutes, until light golden brown and crispy.
6. Repeat step 5 to cook remaining shrimp.

# Beer-breaded Halibut Fish Tacos

Servings: 4
Cooking Time: 10 Minutes

**Ingredients:**

- 1 pound halibut, cut into 1-inch strips
- 1 cup light beer
- 1 jalapeño, minced and divided
- 1 clove garlic, minced
- ¼ teaspoon ground cumin
- ½ cup cornmeal
- ¼ cup all-purpose flour
- 1¼ teaspoons sea salt, divided
- 2 cups shredded cabbage
- 1 lime, juiced and divided
- ¼ cup Greek yogurt
- ¼ cup mayonnaise
- 1 cup grape tomatoes, quartered
- ½ cup chopped cilantro
- ¼ cup chopped onion
- 1 egg, whisked
- 8 corn tortillas

**Directions:**

1. In a shallow baking dish, place the fish, the beer, 1 teaspoon of the minced jalapeño, the garlic, and the cumin. Cover and refrigerate for 30 minutes.
2. Meanwhile, in a medium bowl, mix together the cornmeal, flour, and ½ teaspoon of the salt.
3. In large bowl, mix together the shredded cabbage, 1 tablespoon of the lime juice, the Greek yogurt, the mayonnaise, and ½ teaspoon of the salt.
4. In a small bowl, make the pico de gallo by mixing together the tomatoes, cilantro, onion, ¼ teaspoon of the salt, the remaining jalapeño, and the remaining lime juice.
5. Remove the fish from the refrigerator and discard the marinade. Dredge the fish in the whisked egg; then dredge the fish in the cornmeal flour mixture, until all pieces of fish have been breaded.
6. Preheat the toaster oven to 350°F.
7. Place the fish in the air fryer oven and spray liberally with cooking spray. Air-fry for 6 minutes, flip the fish, and cook another 4 minutes.
8. While the fish is cooking, heat the tortillas in a heavy skillet for 1 to 2 minutes over high heat.
9. To assemble the tacos, place the battered fish on the heated tortillas, and top with slaw and pico de gallo. Serve immediately.

## Sea Scallops

Servings: 4
Cooking Time: 8 Minutes

**Ingredients:**

- 1½ pounds sea scallops
- salt and pepper
- 2 eggs
- ½ cup flour
- ½ cup plain breadcrumbs
- oil for misting or cooking spray

**Directions:**

1. Rinse scallops and remove the tough side muscle. Sprinkle to taste with salt and pepper.
2. Beat eggs together in a shallow dish. Place flour in a second shallow dish and breadcrumbs in a third.
3. Preheat the toaster oven to 390°F.
4. Dip scallops in flour, then eggs, and then roll in breadcrumbs. Mist with oil or cooking spray.
5. Place scallops in air fryer oven in a single layer, leaving some space between. You should be able to cook about a dozen at a time.
6. Air-fry at 390°F for 8 minutes, watching carefully so as not to overcook. Scallops are done when they turn opaque all the way through. They will feel slightly firm when pressed with tines of a fork.
7. Repeat step 6 to cook remaining scallops.

## Quick Shrimp Scampi

Servings: 2
Cooking Time: 5 Minutes

**Ingredients:**

- 16 to 20 raw large shrimp, peeled, deveined and tails removed
- ½ cup white wine
- freshly ground black pepper
- ¼ cup + 1 tablespoon butter, divided
- 1 clove garlic, sliced
- 1 teaspoon olive oil
- salt, to taste
- juice of ½ lemon, to taste
- ¼ cup chopped fresh parsley

**Directions:**

1. Start by marinating the shrimp in the white wine and freshly ground black pepper for at least 30 minutes, or as long as 2 hours in the refrigerator.
2. Preheat the toaster oven to 400°F.
3. Melt ¼ cup of butter in a small saucepan on the stovetop. Add the garlic and let the butter simmer, but be sure to not let it burn.
4. Pour the shrimp and marinade into the air fryer oven, letting the marinade drain through to the bottom drawer. Drizzle the olive oil on the shrimp and season well with salt. Air-fry at 400°F for 3 minutes. Turn the shrimp over and pour the garlic butter over the shrimp. Air-fry for another 2 minutes.
5. Remove the shrimp from the air fryer oven and transfer them to a bowl. Squeeze lemon juice over all the shrimp and toss with the chopped parsley and remaining tablespoon of butter. Season to taste with salt and serve immediately.

## Crunchy Clam Strips

Servings: 3

Cooking Time: 8 Minutes

**Ingredients:**

- ½ pound Clam strips, drained
- 1 Large egg, well beaten
- ½ cup All-purpose flour
- ½ cup Yellow cornmeal
- 1½ teaspoons Table salt
- 1½ teaspoons Ground black pepper
- Up to ¾ teaspoon Cayenne
- Vegetable oil spray

**Directions:**

1. Preheat the toaster oven to 400°F.
2. Toss the clam strips and beaten egg in a bowl until the clams are well coated.
3. Mix the flour, cornmeal, salt, pepper, and cayenne in a large zip-closed plastic bag until well combined. Using a flatware fork or small kitchen tongs, lift the clam strips one by one out of the egg, letting any excess egg slip back into the rest. Put the strips in the bag with the flour mixture. Once all the strips are in the bag, seal it until the strips are well coated.
4. Use kitchen tongs to pick out the clam strips and lay them on a cutting board (leaving any extra flour mixture in the bag to be discarded). Coat the strips on both sides with vegetable oil spray.
5. When the machine is at temperature, spread the clam strips in the air fryer oven in one layer. They may touch in places, but try to leave as much air space as possible around them. Air-fry undisturbed for 8 minutes, or until brown and crunchy.
6. Gently dump the contents of the air fryer oven onto a serving platter. Cool for just a minute or two before serving hot.

## Butternut Squash–wrapped Halibut Fillets

Servings: 3
Cooking Time: 11 Minutes

**Ingredients:**

- 15 Long spiralized peeled and seeded butternut squash strands
- 3 5- to 6-ounce skinless halibut fillets
- 3 tablespoons Butter, melted
- ¾ teaspoon Mild paprika
- ¾ teaspoon Table salt
- ¾ teaspoon Ground black pepper

**Directions:**

1. Preheat the toaster oven to 375°F .
2. Hold 5 long butternut squash strands together and wrap them around a fillet. Set it aside and wrap any remaining fillet(s).
3. Mix the melted butter, paprika, salt, and pepper in a small bowl. Brush this mixture over the squash-wrapped fillets on all sides.
4. When the machine is at temperature, set the fillets in the air fryer oven with as much air space between them as possible. Air-fry undisturbed for 10 minutes, or until the squash strands have browned but not burned. If the machine is at 360°F, you may need to add 1 minute to the cooking time. In any event, watch the fish carefully after the 8-minute mark.
5. Use a nonstick-safe spatula to gently transfer the fillets to a serving platter or plates. Cool for only a minute or so before serving.

## Tilapia Teriyaki

Servings: 3
Cooking Time: 10 Minutes

**Ingredients:**

- 4 tablespoons teriyaki sauce
- 1 tablespoon pineapple juice
- 1 pound tilapia fillets
- cooking spray
- 6 ounces frozen mixed peppers with onions, thawed and drained
- 2 cups cooked rice

**Directions:**

1. Mix the teriyaki sauce and pineapple juice together in a small bowl.
2. Split tilapia fillets down the center lengthwise.
3. Brush all sides of fish with the sauce, spray air fryer oven with nonstick cooking spray, and place fish in the air fryer oven.
4. Stir the peppers and onions into the remaining sauce and spoon over the fish. Save any leftover sauce for drizzling over the fish when serving.
5. Air-fry at 360°F for 10 minutes, until fish flakes easily with a fork and is done in center.
6. Divide into 3 or 4 servings and serve each with approximately ½ cup cooked rice.

## Scallops In Orange Sauce

Servings: 4
Cooking Time: 3 Minutes

**Ingredients:**

- Broiling mixture:
- 1 cup orange juice
- 1 teaspoon soy sauce
- 2 garlic cloves, finely minced
- 1 teaspoon grated orange zest
- 1½ pounds (3 cups) bay scallops, rinsed and drained
- 1 7-ounce can sliced water chestnuts, drained well
- 2 tablespoons chopped watercress

**Directions:**

1. Whisk together the broiling mixture ingredients in a small bowl and transfer to an 8½ × 8½ × 2-inch oiled or nonstick square (cake) pan.
2. BROIL the sauce for 10 minutes to reduce the liquid and meld the flavors. Remove the pan from the oven and add the scallops, spooning the sauce over them.
3. BROIL for 3 minutes, or until opaque. Serve the scallops with the sauce and garnish with the sliced water chestnuts and chopped watercress.

## Lemon-roasted Fish With Olives + Capers

Servings: 4
Cooking Time: 10 Minutes

**Ingredients:**

- Nonstick cooking spray
- 1 pound cod or white-fleshed, mild-flavored fillets, patted dry
- Kosher salt and freshly ground black pepper
- ½ teaspoon paprika
- 1 large lemon
- 3 tablespoons dry white wine
- ½ cup pitted kalamata or other variety olives, drained
- 2 tablespoons capers, drained
- 1 tablespoon olive oil

**Directions:**

1. Preheat the toaster oven to 425°F. Spray a 12 x 12-inch baking pan with nonstick cooking spray.
2. Place the fish fillets on the prepared pan. Season with salt, pepper, and paprika.
3. Slice the lemon in half. Slice one half crosswise into almost paper-thin slices. Arrange the slices evenly over the fish. Juice the remaining half of the lemon and drizzle over the fish. Drizzle the wine over the fish. Top with the olives and capers, then drizzle with the olive oil.
4. Roast for 10 minutes or until the fish flakes easily with a fork and a meat thermometer registers 145°F. To serve, spoon the pan drippings, olives, and capers over the fish.

# Best-dressed Trout

Servings: 2

Cooking Time: 25 Minutes

**Ingredients:**

- 2 dressed trout
- 1 egg, beaten
- 2 tablespoons finely ground almonds
- 2 tablespoons unbleached flour
- 1 teaspoon paprika or smoked paprika
- Pinch of salt (optional)
- 4 lemon slices, approximately ¼ inch thick
- 1 teaspoon lemon juice

**Directions:**

1. Preheat the toaster oven to 400° F.
2. Brush the trout (both sides) with the beaten egg. Blend the almonds, flour, paprika, and salt in a bowl and sprinkle both sides of the trout. Insert 2 lemon slices in each trout cavity and place the trout in an oiled or nonstick 8½ × 8½ × 2-inch square baking (cake) pan.
3. BAKE for 20 minutes, or until the meat is white and firm. Remove from the oven and turn the trout carefully with a spatula.
4. BROIL for 5 minutes, or until the trout is lightly browned.

# BEEF PORK AND LAMB

## Glazed Meatloaf

Servings: 4
Cooking Time: 60 Minutes

**Ingredients:**

- 2 pounds extra-lean ground beef
- ½ cup fine bread crumbs
- 1 large egg
- 1 medium carrot, shredded
- 2 teaspoons minced garlic
- ¼ cup milk
- 1 tablespoon Italian seasoning
- ½ teaspoon sea salt
- ⅛ teaspoon freshly ground black pepper
- ½ cup ketchup
- 1 tablespoon dark brown sugar
- 1 teaspoon apple cider vinegar

**Directions:**

1. Place the rack in position 1 and preheat the toaster oven to 375°F on BAKE for 5 minutes.
2. In a large bowl, mix the ground beef, bread crumbs, egg, carrot, garlic, milk, Italian seasoning, salt, and pepper until well combined.
3. Press the mixture into a 9-by-5-inch loaf pan.
4. In a small bowl, stir the ketchup, brown sugar, and vinegar. Set aside.
5. Bake for 40 minutes.
6. Take the meatloaf out and spread the glaze over the top. Bake an additional 20 minutes until cooked through, with an internal temperature of 165°F. Serve.

# Zesty London Broil

Servings: 4

Cooking Time: 28 Minutes

**Ingredients:**

- ⅔ cup ketchup
- ¼ cup honey
- ¼ cup olive oil
- 2 tablespoons apple cider vinegar
- 2 tablespoons Worcestershire sauce
- 2 tablespoons minced onion
- ½ teaspoon paprika
- 1 teaspoon salt
- 1 teaspoon freshly ground black pepper
- 2 pounds London broil, top round or flank steak (about 1-inch thick)

**Directions:**

1. Combine the ketchup, honey, olive oil, apple cider vinegar, Worcestershire sauce, minced onion, paprika, salt and pepper in a small bowl and whisk together.
2. Generously pierce both sides of the meat with a fork or meat tenderizer and place it in a shallow dish. Pour the marinade mixture over the steak, making sure all sides of the meat get coated with the marinade. Cover and refrigerate overnight.
3. Preheat the toaster oven to 400°F.
4. Transfer the London broil to the air fryer oven and air-fry for 28 minutes, depending on how rare or well done you like your steak. Flip the steak over halfway through the cooking time.
5. Remove the London broil from the air fryer oven and let it rest for five minutes on a cutting board. To serve, thinly slice the meat against the grain and transfer to a serving platter.

# Ribeye Steak With Blue Cheese Compound Butter

Servings: 2

Cooking Time: 12 Minutes

**Ingredients:**

- 5 tablespoons unsalted butter, softened
- ¼ cup crumbled blue cheese 2 teaspoons lemon juice
- 1 tablespoon freshly chopped chives
- Salt & freshly ground black pepper, to taste
- 2 (12 ounce) boneless ribeye steaks

**Directions:**

1. Mix together butter, blue cheese, lemon juice, and chives until smooth.
2. Season the butter to taste with salt and pepper.
3. Place the butter on plastic wrap and form into a 3-inch log, tying the ends of the plastic wrap together.
4. Place the butter in the fridge for 4 hours to harden.
5. Allow the steaks to sit at room temperature for 1 hour.
6. Pat the steaks dry with paper towels and season to taste with salt and pepper.
7. Insert the fry basket at top position in the Cosori Smart Air Fryer Toaster Oven.
8. Preheat the toaster Oven to 450°F.
9. Place the steaks in the fry basket in the preheated oven.
10. Select the Broil function, adjust time to 12 minutes, and press Start/Pause.
11. Remove when done and allow to rest for 5 minutes.
12. Remove the butter from the fridge, unwrap, and slice into ¾-inch pieces.
13. Serve the steak with one or two pieces of sliced compound butter.

# Meatloaf With Tangy Tomato Glaze

Servings: 6

Cooking Time: 50 Minutes

**Ingredients:**

- 1 pound ground beef
- ½ pound ground pork
- ½ pound ground veal (or turkey)
- 1 medium onion, diced
- 1 small clove of garlic, minced
- 2 egg yolks, lightly beaten
- ½ cup tomato ketchup
- 1 tablespoon Worcestershire sauce
- ½ cup plain breadcrumbs
- 2 teaspoons salt
- freshly ground black pepper
- ½ cup chopped fresh parsley, plus more for garnish
- 6 tablespoons ketchup
- 1 tablespoon balsamic vinegar
- 2 tablespoons brown sugar

**Directions:**

1. Combine the meats, onion, garlic, egg yolks, ketchup, Worcestershire sauce, breadcrumbs, salt, pepper and fresh parsley in a large bowl and mix well.
2. Preheat the toaster oven to 350°F and pour a little water into the bottom of the air fryer oven. (This will help prevent the grease that drips into the bottom drawer from burning and smoking.)
3. Transfer the meatloaf mixture to the air fryer oven, packing it down gently. Run a spatula around the meatloaf to create a space about ½-inch wide between the meat and the side of the air fryer oven.
4. Air-fry at 350°F for 20 minutes. Carefully invert the meatloaf onto a plate (remember to remove the pan from the air fryer oven so you don't pour all the grease out) and slide it back into the air fryer oven to turn it over. Re-shape the meatloaf with a spatula if necessary. Air-fry for another 20 minutes at 350°F.
5. Combine the ketchup, balsamic vinegar and brown sugar in a bowl and spread the mixture over the meatloaf. Air-fry for another 10 minutes, until an instant read thermometer inserted into the center of the meatloaf registers 160°F.
6. Allow the meatloaf to rest for a few more minutes and then transfer it to a serving platter using a spatula. Slice the meatloaf, sprinkle a little chopped parsley on top if desired, and serve.

# Orange Glazed Pork Tenderloin

Servings: 3
Cooking Time: 23 Minutes

**Ingredients:**

- 2 tablespoons brown sugar
- 2 teaspoons cornstarch
- 2 teaspoons Dijon mustard
- ½ cup orange juice
- ½ teaspoon soy sauce
- 2 teaspoons grated fresh ginger
- ¼ cup white wine
- zest of 1 orange
- 1 pound pork tenderloin
- salt and freshly ground black pepper
- oranges, halved (for garnish)
- fresh parsley or other green herb (for garnish)

**Directions:**

1. Combine the brown sugar, cornstarch, Dijon mustard, orange juice, soy sauce, ginger, white wine and orange zest in a small saucepan and bring the mixture to a boil on the stovetop. Lower the heat and simmer while you cook the pork tenderloin or until the sauce has thickened.
2. Preheat the toaster oven to 370°F.
3. Season all sides of the pork tenderloin with salt and freshly ground black pepper. Transfer the tenderloin to the air fryer oven, bending the pork into a wide "U" shape if necessary to fit in the air fryer oven. Air-fry at 370°F for 20 to 23 minutes, or until the internal temperature reaches 145°F. Flip the tenderloin over halfway through the cooking process and baste with the sauce.
4. Transfer the tenderloin to a cutting board and let it rest for 5 minutes. Slice the pork at a slight angle and serve immediately with orange halves and fresh herbs to dress it up. Drizzle any remaining glaze over the top.

## Herbed Lamb Burgers

Servings: 4
Cooking Time: 15 Minutes

**Ingredients:**

- 1 pound lean ground lamb
- 1 large egg
- 1 tablespoon fresh parsley, chopped
- 2 teaspoons fresh mint, chopped
- 1 teaspoon minced garlic
- ¼ teaspoon sea salt
- ⅛ teaspoon freshly ground black pepper
- Olive oil spray (hand-pumped)
- 4 whole-wheat buns
- ¼ cup store-bought tzatziki sauce
- 1 tomato, cut into slices
- 4 thin red onion slices
- ½ cup shredded lettuce

**Directions:**

1. Preheat the toaster oven to 350°F on CONVECTION BROIL for 5 minutes.
2. In a large bowl, mix the lamb, egg, parsley, mint, garlic, salt, and pepper. Form the mixture into 4 patties.
3. Place the air-fryer basket in the baking tray and place the burger patties in the basket. Lightly spray the patties with the oil on both sides.
4. In position 2, broil for 15 minutes, turning halfway through.
5. Serve on the buns topped with tzatziki sauce, tomato, onion, and lettuce.

## Beef Vegetable Stew

Servings: 4
Cooking Time: 120 Minutes

**Ingredients:**

- 1 pound lean stewing beef, cut into 1-inch chunks
- 2 carrots, diced
- 2 celery stalks
- 1 large potato, diced
- ½ sweet onion, chopped
- 2 teaspoons minced garlic
- 1 (15-ounce) can diced tomatoes, with juices
- 1 teaspoon sea salt
- ½ teaspoon freshly ground black pepper
- 1 cup low-sodium beef broth
- 3 tablespoons all-purpose flour
- 1 cup frozen peas

**Directions:**

1. Place the rack in position 1 and preheat the toaster oven to 375°F on BAKE for 5 minutes.
2. In a 1½-quart casserole dish, combine the beef, carrots, celery, potato, onion, garlic, tomatoes, salt, and pepper.
3. In a small bowl, stir the broth and flour until well combined. Add the broth mixture to the beef mixture and stir to combine.
4. Cover with foil or a lid and bake for 2 hours, stirring each time you reset the timer, until the meat is very tender.
5. Stir in the peas and let stand for 10 minutes. Serve.

## Italian Sausage & Peppers

Servings: 6
Cooking Time: 25 Minutes

**Ingredients:**

- 1 6-ounce can tomato paste
- ⅔ cup water
- 1 8-ounce can tomato sauce
- 1 teaspoon dried parsley flakes
- ½ teaspoon garlic powder
- ⅛ teaspoon oregano
- ½ pound mild Italian bulk sausage
- 1 tablespoon extra virgin olive oil
- ½ large onion, cut in 1-inch chunks
- 4 ounces fresh mushrooms, sliced
- 1 large green bell pepper, cut in 1-inch chunks
- 8 ounces spaghetti, cooked
- Parmesan cheese for serving

**Directions:**

1. In a large saucepan or skillet, stir together the tomato paste, water, tomato sauce, parsley, garlic, and oregano. Heat on stovetop over very low heat while preparing meat and vegetables.
2. Break sausage into small chunks, about ½-inch pieces. Place in air fryer oven baking pan.
3. Air-fry at 390°F for 5 minutes. Stir. Cook 7 minutes longer or until sausage is well done. Remove from pan, drain on paper towels, and add to the sauce mixture.
4. If any sausage grease remains in baking pan, pour it off or use paper towels to soak it up. (Be careful handling that hot pan!)
5. Place olive oil, onions, and mushrooms in pan and stir. Air-fry for 5 minutes or just until tender. Using a slotted spoon, transfer onions and mushrooms from baking pan into the sauce and sausage mixture.
6. Place bell pepper chunks in air fryer oven baking pan and air-fry for 8 minutes or until tender. When done, stir into sauce with sausage and other vegetables.
7. Serve over cooked spaghetti with plenty of Parmesan cheese.

## Bourbon Broiled Steak

Servings: 2
Cooking Time: 14 Minutes

**Ingredients:**

- Brushing mixture:
- ¼ cup bourbon
- 1 teaspoon garlic powder
- 1 tablespoon olive oil
- 1 teaspoon soy sauce
- 2 6- to 8-ounce sirloin steaks, ¾ inch thick

**Directions:**

1. Combine the brushing mixture ingredients in a small bowl. Brush the steaks on both sides with the mixture and place on the broiling rack with a pan underneath.
2. BROIL 4 minutes, remove from the oven, turn with tongs, brush the top and sides, and broil again for 4 minutes, or until done to your preference. To use the brushing mixture as a sauce or gravy, pour the mixture into a baking pan.
3. BROIL the mixture for 6 minutes, or until it begins to bubble.

# Steak Pinwheels With Pepper Slaw And Minneapolis Potato Salad

Servings: 4

Cooking Time: 16 Minutes

**Ingredients:**

- Brushing mixture:
- ½ cup cold strong brewed coffee
- 2 tablespoons molasses
- 1 tablespoon tomato paste
- 2 garlic cloves, minced
- 1 tablespoon olive oil
- Garlic powder
- 1 teaspoon butcher's pepper
- 1 pound lean, boneless beefsteak, flattened to ⅛-inch thickness with a meat mallet or rolling pin (place steak between 2 sheets of heavy-duty plastic wrap)

**Directions:**

1. Combine the brushing mixture ingredients in a small bowl and set aside.
2. Cut the steak into 2 × 3-inch strips, brush with the mixture, and roll up, securing the edges with toothpicks. Brush again with the mixture and place in an oiled or nonstick 8½ × 8½ × 2-inch square baking (cake) pan.
3. BROIL for 8 minutes, then turn with tongs, brush with the mixture again, and broil for another 8 minutes, or until browned.

## Barbecue-style London Broil

Servings: 5

Cooking Time: 17 Minutes

**Ingredients:**

- ¾ teaspoon Mild smoked paprika
- ¾ teaspoon Dried oregano
- ¾ teaspoon Table salt
- ¾ teaspoon Ground black pepper
- ¼ teaspoon Garlic powder
- ¼ teaspoon Onion powder
- 1½ pounds Beef London broil (in one piece)
- Olive oil spray

**Directions:**

1. Preheat the toaster oven to 400°F.
2. Mix the smoked paprika, oregano, salt, pepper, garlic powder, and onion powder in a small bowl until uniform.
3. Pat and rub this mixture across all surfaces of the beef. Lightly coat the beef on all sides with olive oil spray.
4. When the machine is at temperature, lay the London broil flat in the air fryer oven and air-fry undisturbed for 8 minutes for the small batch, 10 minutes for the medium batch, or 12 minutes for the large batch for medium-rare, until an instant-read meat thermometer inserted into the center of the meat registers 130°F (not USDA-approved). Add 1, 2, or 3 minutes, respectively (based on the size of the cut) for medium, until an instant-read meat thermometer registers 135°F (not USDA-approved). Or add 3, 4, or 5 minutes respectively for medium, until an instant-read meat thermometer registers 145°F (USDA-approved).
5. Use kitchen tongs to transfer the London broil to a cutting board. Let the meat rest for 10 minutes. It needs a long time for the juices to be reincorporated into the meat's fibers. Carve it against the grain into very thin (less than ¼-inch-thick) slices to serve.

## Kielbasa Sausage With Pierogies And Caramelized Onions

Servings: 3
Cooking Time: 30 Minutes

**Ingredients:**

- 1 Vidalia or sweet onion, sliced
- olive oil
- salt and freshly ground black pepper
- 2 tablespoons butter, cut into small cubes
- 1 teaspoon sugar
- 1 pound light Polish kielbasa sausage, cut into 2-inch chunks
- 1 (13-ounce) package frozen mini pierogies
- 2 teaspoons vegetable or olive oil
- chopped scallions

**Directions:**

1. Preheat the toaster oven to 400°F.
2. Toss the sliced onions with a little olive oil, salt and pepper and transfer them to the air fryer oven. Dot the onions with pieces of butter and air-fry at 400°F for 2 minutes. Then sprinkle the sugar over the onions and stir. Pour any melted butter from the bottom of the air fryer oven over the onions (do this over the sink – some of the butter will spill through the pan). Continue to air-fry for another 13 minutes, stirring the pan every few minutes to cook the onions evenly.
3. Add the kielbasa chunks to the onions and toss. Air-fry for another 5 minutes. Transfer the kielbasa and onions to a bowl and cover with aluminum foil to keep warm.
4. Toss the frozen pierogies with the vegetable or olive oil and transfer them to the air fryer oven. Air-fry at 400°F for 8 minutes.
5. When the pierogies have finished cooking, return the kielbasa and onions to the air fryer oven and gently toss with the pierogies. Air-fry for 2 more minutes and then transfer everything to a serving platter. Garnish with the chopped scallions and serve hot with the spicy sour cream sauce below.
6. Kielbasa Sausage with Pierogies and Caramelized Onions

## Spicy Little Beef Birds

Servings: 2
Cooking Time: 12 Minutes

**Ingredients:**

- Spicy mixture:
- 1 tablespoon olive oil
- 1 tablespoon brown mustard
- 1 teaspoon chili powder
- 1 teaspoon garlic powder
- 1 teaspoon hot sauce
- 1 tablespoon barbecue sauce or salsa
- Salt and freshly ground black pepper to taste
- ½ to ¾ pound pepper steaks, cut into 3 × 4-inch strips

**Directions:**

1. Blend the spicy mixture ingredients in a small bowl and brush both sides of the beef strips.
2. Roll up the strips lengthwise and fasten with toothpicks near each end. Place the beef rolls in an oiled or nonstick 8½ × 8½ × 2-inch square baking (cake) pan.
3. BROIL for 6 minutes, remove from the oven, and turn with tongs. Brush with the spicy mixture and broil again for 6 minutes, or until done to your preference.

# Pretzel-coated Pork Tenderloin

Servings: 4

Cooking Time: 10 Minutes

**Ingredients:**

- 1 Large egg white(s)
- 2 teaspoons Dijon mustard (gluten-free, if a concern)
- 1½ cups (about 6 ounces) Crushed pretzel crumbs
- 1 pound (4 sections) Pork tenderloin, cut into ¼-pound (4-ounce) sections
- Vegetable oil spray

**Directions:**

1. Preheat the toaster oven to 350°F .
2. Set up and fill two shallow soup plates or small pie plates on your counter: one for the egg white(s), whisked with the mustard until foamy; and one for the pretzel crumbs.
3. Dip a section of pork tenderloin in the egg white mixture and turn it to coat well, even on the ends. Let any excess egg white mixture slip back into the rest, then set the pork in the pretzel crumbs. Roll it several times, pressing gently, until the pork is evenly coated, even on the ends. Generously coat the pork section with vegetable oil spray, set it aside, and continue coating and spraying the remaining sections.
4. Set the pork sections in the air fryer oven with at least ¼ inch between them. Air-fry undisturbed for 10 minutes, or until an instant-read meat thermometer inserted into the center of one section registers 145°F.
5. Use kitchen tongs to transfer the pieces to a wire rack. Cool for 3 to 5 minutes before serving.

## Air-fried Roast Beef With Rosemary Roasted Potatoes

Servings: 8
Cooking Time: 60 Minutes

**Ingredients:**

- 1 (5-pound) top sirloin roast
- salt and freshly ground black pepper
- 1 teaspoon dried thyme
- 2 pounds red potatoes, halved or quartered
- 2 teaspoons olive oil
- 1 teaspoon very finely chopped fresh rosemary, plus more for garnish

**Directions:**

1. Start by making sure your roast will fit into the air fryer oven without touching the top element. Trim it if you have to in order to get it to fit nicely in your air fryer oven. (You can always save the trimmings for another use, like a beef sandwich.)
2. Preheat the toaster oven to 360°F.
3. Season the beef all over with salt, pepper and thyme. Transfer the seasoned roast to the air fryer oven.
4. Air-fry at 360°F for 20 minutes. Turn the roast over and continue to air-fry at 360°F for another 20 minutes.
5. Toss the potatoes with the olive oil, salt, pepper and fresh rosemary. Turn the roast over again in the air fryer oven and toss the potatoes in around the sides of the roast. Air-fry the roast and potatoes at 360°F for another 20 minutes. Check the internal temperature of the roast with an instant-read thermometer, and continue to roast until the beef is 5° lower than your desired degree of doneness. (Rare – 130°F, Medium – 150°F, Well done – 170°F.) Let the roast rest for 5 to 10 minutes before slicing and serving. While the roast is resting, continue to air-fry the potatoes if desired for extra browning and crispiness.
6. Slice the roast and serve with the potatoes, adding a little more fresh rosemary if desired.

## Traditional Pot Roast

Servings: 6
Cooking Time: 75 Minutes

**Ingredients:**

- 2 tablespoons olive oil
- 1 teaspoon garlic powder
- 1 teaspoon fresh thyme, chopped
- ¼ teaspoon sea salt
- ¼ teaspoon freshly ground black pepper
- 1 (3-pound) beef rump roast

**Directions:**

1. Preheat the toaster oven to 350°F on CONVECTION BAKE for 5 minutes.
2. In a small bowl, stir the oil, garlic, thyme, salt, and pepper. Spread the mixture all over the beef.
3. Place the air-fryer basket in the baking tray and place the beef in the basket.
4. In position 1, bake for 1 hour and 15 minutes until browned and the internal temperature reaches 145°F for medium.
5. Let the roast rest 10 minutes and serve.

# Spanish Pork Skewers

Servings: 4

Cooking Time: 16 Minutes

**Ingredients:**

- 1 pound pork tenderloin, cut into ¾- to 1-inch cubes
- 2 tablespoons olive oil
- 1 teaspoon ground cumin
- ½ teaspoon smoked paprika
- ½ teaspoon dried thyme leaves
- ½ teaspoon kosher salt, plus more for seasoning
- ⅛ teaspoon red pepper flakes
- 2 cloves garlic, minced
- 1 red bell pepper, cut into ¾- to 1-inch squares
- 1 small red onion, cut into ¾- to 1-inch wedges
- Freshly ground black pepper
- Nonstick cooking spray
- 2 tablespoons unsalted butter
- 1 tablespoon sherry or balsamic vinegar
- 1 teaspoon packed dark brown sugar

**Directions:**

1. Place the pork cubes in a medium bowl. Drizzle 1 tablespoon of oil over the pork. Stir the cumin, paprika, thyme, ½ teaspoon salt, the pepper flakes, and garlic in a small bowl. Sprinkle the seasonings over the pork. Stir to coat the pork evenly. Cover and refrigerate for at least 4 hours or up to overnight.
2. Place the bell pepper and onion pieces in a medium bowl. Drizzle with the remaining tablespoon olive oil and season with salt and pepper. Toss to coat evenly.
3. Alternately thread the pork and vegetables onto skewers. Spray a 12 x 12-inch baking pan with nonstick cooking spray. Place the filled skewers on the prepared pan. Place the pan in the toaster oven, positioning the skewers about 3 to 4 inches below the heating element. (Depending on your oven, you may need to set the rack to the middle position.)
4. Set the toaster oven on broil. Broil for 10 minutes. Turn the skewers. Broil for an additional 5 minutes, or until the vegetables are tender and a meat thermometer registers 145°F. Do not overcook.
5. Meanwhile, combine the butter, vinegar, and brown sugar in a small, glass, microwave-safe bowl. Season with salt and pepper. Microwave on High (100 percent) power for 45 seconds or until the butter melts and the mixture begins to bubble. Stir to dissolve the sugar.
6. Lightly brush the vinegar mixture over the skewers. Broil for 1 minute or until the skewers are browned.

# Vietnamese Beef Lettuce Wraps

Servings: 4
Cooking Time: 12 Minutes

**Ingredients:**

- ⅓ cup low-sodium soy sauce
- 2 teaspoons fish sauce
- 2 teaspoons brown sugar
- 1 tablespoon chili paste
- juice of 1 lime
- 2 cloves garlic, minced
- 2 teaspoons fresh ginger, minced
- 1 pound beef sirloin
- Sauce
- ⅓ cup low-sodium soy sauce
- juice of 2 limes
- 1 tablespoon mirin wine
- 2 teaspoons chili paste
- Serving
- 1 head butter lettuce
- ½ cup julienned carrots
- ½ cup julienned cucumber
- ½ cup sliced radishes, sliced into half moons
- 2 cups cooked rice noodles
- ⅓ cup chopped peanuts

**Directions:**

1. Combine the soy sauce, fish sauce, brown sugar, chili paste, lime juice, garlic and ginger in a bowl. Slice the beef into thin slices, then cut those slices in half. Add the beef to the marinade and marinate for 1 to 3 hours in the refrigerator. When you are ready to cook, remove the steak from the refrigerator and let it sit at room temperature for 30 minutes.
2. Preheat the toaster oven to 400°F.
3. Transfer the beef and marinade to the air fryer oven. Air-fry at 400°F for 12 minutes.
4. While the beef is cooking, prepare a wrap-building station. Combine the soy sauce, lime juice, mirin wine and chili paste in a bowl and transfer to a little pouring vessel. Separate the lettuce leaves from the head of lettuce and put them in a serving bowl. Place the carrots, cucumber, radish, rice noodles and chopped peanuts all in separate serving bowls.
5. When the beef has finished cooking, transfer it to another serving bowl and invite your guests to build their wraps. To build the wraps, place some beef in a lettuce leaf and top with carrots, cucumbers, some rice noodles and chopped peanuts. Drizzle a little sauce over top, fold the lettuce around the ingredients and enjoy!

# Lamb Burger With Feta And Olives

Servings: 3
Cooking Time: 16 Minutes

**Ingredients:**

- 2 teaspoons olive oil
- ⅓ onion, finely chopped
- 1 clove garlic, minced
- 1 pound ground lamb
- 2 tablespoons fresh parsley, finely chopped
- 1½ teaspoons fresh oregano, finely chopped
- ½ cup black olives, finely chopped
- ⅓ cup crumbled feta cheese
- ½ teaspoon salt
- freshly ground black pepper
- 4 thick pita breads
- toppings and condiments

**Directions:**

1. Preheat a medium skillet over medium-high heat on the stovetop. Add the olive oil and cook the onion until tender, but not browned – about 4 to 5 minutes. Add the garlic and air-fry for another minute. Transfer the onion and garlic to a mixing bowl and add the ground lamb, parsley, oregano, olives, feta cheese, salt and pepper. Gently mix the ingredients together.
2. Divide the mixture into 3 or 4 equal portions and then form the hamburgers, being careful not to over-handle the meat. One good way to do this is to throw the meat back and forth between your hands like a baseball, packing the meat each time you catch it. Flatten the balls into patties, making an indentation in the center of each patty. Flatten the sides of the patties as well to make it easier to fit them into the air fryer oven.
3. Preheat the toaster oven to 370°F.
4. If you don't have room for all four burgers, air-fry two or three burgers at a time for 8 minutes at 370°F. Flip the burgers over and air-fry for another 8 minutes. If you cooked your burgers in batches, return the first batch of burgers to the air fryer oven for the last two minutes of cooking to re-heat. This should give you a medium-well burger. If you'd prefer a medium-rare burger, shorten the cooking time to about 13 minutes. Remove the burgers to a resting plate and let the burgers rest for a few minutes before dressing and serving.
5. While the burgers are resting, toast the pita breads in the air fryer oven for 2 minutes. Tuck the burgers into the toasted pita breads, or wrap the pitas around the burgers and serve with a tzatziki sauce or some mayonnaise.

# VEGETABLES AND VEGETARIAN

## Hasselback Garlic-and-butter Potatoes

Servings: 3

Cooking Time: 48 Minutes

**Ingredients:**

- 3 8-ounce russet potatoes
- 6 Brown button or Baby Bella mushrooms, very thinly sliced
- Olive oil spray
- 3 tablespoons Butter, melted and cooled
- 1 tablespoon Minced garlic
- ¾ teaspoon Table salt
- 3 tablespoons (about ½ ounce) Finely grated Parmesan cheese

**Directions:**

1. Preheat the toaster oven to 350°F .
2. Cut slits down the length of each potato, about three-quarters down into the potato and spaced about ¼ inch apart. Wedge a thin mushroom slice in each slit. Generously coat the potatoes on all sides with olive oil spray.
3. When the machine is at temperature, set the potatoes mushroom side up in the air fryer oven with as much air space between them as possible. Air-fry undisturbed for 45 minutes, or tender when pricked with a fork.
4. Increase the machine's temperature to 400°F. Use kitchen tongs, and perhaps a flatware fork for balance, to gently transfer the potatoes to a cutting board. Brush each evenly with butter, then sprinkle the minced garlic and salt over them. Sprinkle the cheese evenly over the potatoes.
5. Use those same tongs to gently transfer the potatoes cheese side up to the air fryer oven in one layer with some space for air flow between them. Air-fry undisturbed for 3 minutes, or until the cheese has melted and begun to brown.
6. Use those same tongs to gently transfer the potatoes back to the wire rack. Cool for 5 minutes before serving.

## Spicy Sweet Potatoes

Servings: 4

Cooking Time: 25 Minutes

**Ingredients:**

- 2 sweet potatoes, peeled and sliced into 1-inch rounds
- 1 tablespoon vegetable oil
- Seasonings:
- ½ teaspoon each: grated nutmeg, ground cinnamon, cardamom, and ginger
- Salt and freshly ground black pepper to taste

**Directions:**

1. Preheat the toaster oven to 400° F.
2. Brush the potato slices with oil and set aside.
3. Combine the seasonings in a 1-quart 8½ × 8½ × 4-inch ovenproof baking dish and add the potato slices. Toss to coat well and adjust the seasonings to taste. Cover the dish with aluminum foil.
4. BAKE for 25 minutes, or until the potatoes are tender.

## Fried Okra

Servings: 4

Cooking Time: 8 Minutes

**Ingredients:**

- 1 pound okra
- 1 large egg
- 1 tablespoon milk
- 1 teaspoon salt, divided
- ½ teaspoon black pepper, divided
- ¼ teaspoon paprika
- ¼ teaspoon thyme
- ½ cup cornmeal
- ½ cup all-purpose flour

**Directions:**

1. Preheat the toaster oven to 400°F.
2. Cut the okra into ½-inch rounds.
3. In a medium bowl, whisk together the egg, milk, ½ teaspoon of the salt, and ¼ teaspoon of black pepper. Place the okra into the egg mixture and toss until well coated.
4. In a separate bowl, mix together the remaining ½ teaspoon of salt, the remaining ¼ teaspoon of black pepper, the paprika, the thyme, the cornmeal, and the flour. Working in small batches, dredge the egg-coated okra in the cornmeal mixture until all the okra has been breaded.
5. Place a single layer of okra in the air fryer oven and spray with cooking spray. Air-fry for 4 minutes, toss to check for crispness, and cook another 4 minutes. Repeat in batches, as needed.

# Parmesan Asparagus

Servings: 2
Cooking Time: 5 Minutes

**Ingredients:**

- 1 bunch asparagus, stems trimmed
- 1 teaspoon olive oil
- salt and freshly ground black pepper
- ¼ cup coarsely grated Parmesan cheese
- ½ lemon

**Directions:**

1. Preheat the toaster oven to 400°F.
2. Toss the asparagus with the oil and season with salt and freshly ground black pepper.
3. Transfer the asparagus to the air fryer oven and air-fry at 400°F for 5 minutes, turn the asparagus once or twice during the cooking process.
4. When the asparagus is cooked to your liking, sprinkle the asparagus generously with the Parmesan cheese and close the air fryer oven again. Let the asparagus sit for 1 minute in the turned-off air fryer oven. Then, remove the asparagus, transfer it to a serving dish and finish with a grind of black pepper and a squeeze of lemon juice.

# Crispy Noodle Salad

Servings: 3
Cooking Time: 22 Minutes

**Ingredients:**

- 6 ounces Fresh Chinese-style stir-fry or lo mein wheat noodles
- 1½ tablespoons Cornstarch
- ¾ cup Chopped stemmed and cored red bell pepper
- 2 Medium scallion(s), trimmed and thinly sliced
- 2 teaspoons Sambal oelek or other pulpy hot red pepper sauce
- 2 teaspoons Thai sweet chili sauce or red ketchup-likc chili sauce, such as Heinz
- 2 teaspoons Regular or low-sodium soy sauce or tamari sauce
- 2 teaspoons Unseasoned rice vinegar
- 1 tablespoon White or black sesame seeds

**Directions:**

1. Bring a large saucepan of water to a boil over high heat. Add the noodles and boil for 2 minutes. Drain in a colander set in the sink. Rinse several times with cold water, shaking the colander to drain the noodles very well. Spread the noodles out on a large cutting board and air-dry for 10 minutes.
2. Preheat the toaster oven to 400°F.
3. Toss the noodles in a bowl with the cornstarch until well coated. Spread them out across the entire air fryer oven (although they will be touching and overlapping a bit). Air-fry for 6 minutes, then turn the solid mass of noodles over as one piece. If it cracks in half or smaller pieces, just fit these back together after turning. Continue air-frying for 6 minutes, or until golden brown and crisp.
4. As the noodles cook, stir the bell pepper, scallion(s), sambal oelek, red chili sauce, soy sauce, vinegar, and sesame seeds in a serving bowl until well combined.
5. Turn the air fryer oven of noodles out onto a cutting board and cool for a minute or two. Break the mass of noodles into individual noodles and/or small chunks and add to the dressing in the serving bowl. Toss well to serve.

## Mushrooms

Servings: 4

Cooking Time: 12 Minutes

**Ingredients:**

- 8 ounces whole white button mushrooms
- ½ teaspoon salt
- ⅛ teaspoon pepper
- ¼ teaspoon garlic powder
- ¼ teaspoon onion powder
- 5 tablespoons potato starch
- 1 egg, beaten
- ¾ cup panko breadcrumbs
- oil for misting or cooking spray

**Directions:**

1. Place mushrooms in a large bowl. Add the salt, pepper, garlic and onion powders, and stir well to distribute seasonings.
2. Add potato starch to mushrooms and toss in bowl until well coated.
3. Dip mushrooms in beaten egg, roll in panko crumbs, and mist with oil or cooking spray.
4. Place mushrooms in air fryer oven. You can cook them all at once, and it's okay if a few are stacked.
5. Air-fry at 390°F for 5 minutes. Rotate, then continue cooking for 7 more minutes, until golden brown and crispy.

## Honey-roasted Parsnips

Servings: 3

Cooking Time: 23 Minutes

**Ingredients:**

- 1½ pounds Medium parsnips, peeled
- Olive oil spray
- 1 tablespoon Honey
- 1½ teaspoons Water
- ¼ teaspoon Table salt

**Directions:**

1. Preheat the toaster oven to 350°F .
2. If the thick end of a parsnip is more than ½ inch in diameter, cut the parsnip just below where it swells to its large end, then slice the large section in half lengthwise. Generously coat the parsnips on all sides with olive oil spray.
3. When the machine is at temperature, set the parsnips in the air fryer oven with as much air space between them as possible. Air-fry undisturbed for 20 minutes.
4. Whisk the honey, water, and salt in a small bowl until smooth. Brush this mixture over the parsnips. Air-fry undisturbed for 3 minutes more, or until the glaze is lightly browned.
5. Use kitchen tongs to transfer the parsnips to a wire rack or a serving platter. Cool for a couple of minutes before serving.

## Potatoes Au Gratin

Servings: 4

Cooking Time: 40 Minutes

**Ingredients:**

- Mixture:
- ½ cup fat-free half-and-half
- ¼ cup nonfat plain yogurt
- 2 tablespoons margarine
- 2 tablespoons unbleached flour
- 1 teaspoon garlic powder
- ¼ cup shredded low-fat mozzarella cheese
- 2 tablespoons grated Parmesan cheese
- Salt and butcher's pepper to taste
- 2 cups peeled and diced potatoes
- ½ cup chopped onion
- 1 tablespoon fresh or frozen chives
- ¼ teaspoon paprika

**Directions:**

1. Preheat the toaster oven to 400° F.
2. Process the mixture ingredients in a food processor or blender until smooth. Pour into a 1-quart 8½ × 8½ × 4-inch ovenproof baking dish.
3. Add the potatoes, onion, chives, and paprika and stir to mix well. Cover the dish with aluminum foil.
4. BAKE, covered, for 40 minutes, or until the potatoes and onion are tender.

## Green Beans

Servings: 4

Cooking Time: 12 Minutes

**Ingredients:**

- 1 pound fresh green beans
- 2 tablespoons Italian salad dressing
- salt and pepper

**Directions:**

1. Wash beans and snap off stem ends.
2. In a large bowl, toss beans with Italian dressing.
3. Air-fry at 330°F for 5 minutes. Stir and cook 5 minutes longer. If needed, continue cooking for 2 minutes, until as tender as you like. Beans should shrivel slightly and brown in places.
4. Sprinkle with salt and pepper to taste.

## Mushrooms, Sautéed

Servings: 4
Cooking Time: 4 Minutes

**Ingredients:**

- 8 ounces sliced white mushrooms, rinsed and well drained
- ¼ teaspoon garlic powder
- 1 tablespoon Worcestershire sauce

**Directions:**

1. Place mushrooms in a large bowl and sprinkle with garlic powder and Worcestershire. Stir well to distribute seasonings evenly.
2. Place in air fryer oven and air-fry at 390°F for 4 minutes, until tender.

## Five-spice Roasted Sweet Potatoes

Servings: 4
Cooking Time: 12 Minutes

**Ingredients:**

- ½ teaspoon ground cinnamon
- ¼ teaspoon ground cumin
- ¼ teaspoon paprika
- 1 teaspoon chile powder
- ⅛ teaspoon turmeric
- ½ teaspoon salt (optional)
- freshly ground black pepper
- 2 large sweet potatoes, peeled and cut into ¾-inch cubes (about 3 cups)
- 1 tablespoon olive oil

**Directions:**

1. In a large bowl, mix together cinnamon, cumin, paprika, chile powder, turmeric, salt, and pepper to taste.
2. Add potatoes and stir well.
3. Drizzle the seasoned potatoes with the olive oil and stir until evenly coated.
4. Place seasoned potatoes in the air fryer oven baking pan or an ovenproof dish that fits inside your air fryer oven.
5. Air-fry for 6 minutes at 390°F, stop, and stir well.
6. Air-fry for an additional 6 minutes.

# Lentil-stuffed Zucchini

Servings: 2

Cooking Time: 50 Minutes

**Ingredients:**

- 2 large zucchini
- 2 teaspoons olive oil
- 1 (15-ounce) can low-sodium lentils, drained and rinsed
- 1 large tomato, chopped
- 1 scallion, both white and green parts, chopped
- ½ jalapeño pepper, minced
- ½ cup corn kernels, fresh or frozen (thawed)
- 1 tablespoon fresh cilantro, chopped
- 1 teaspoon minced garlic
- 1 teaspoon ground cumin
- ¼ teaspoon chili powder
- ½ cup shredded Monterey Jack cheese

**Directions:**

1. Preheat the toaster oven to 400°F on BAKE for 5 minutes.
2. Line the baking tray with parchment paper.
3. Cut the zucchini in half lengthwise and scoop out the insides so that you have a hollow shell (about ¼-inch thick all the way around).
4. Lightly oil both sides of the zucchini shells and set them on the baking sheet.
5. In a large bowl, stir the lentils, tomato, scallion, jalapeño, corn, cilantro, garlic, cumin, and chili powder until well mixed.
6. Spoon the lentil mixture into the zucchini and top with the cheese.
7. Bake for 50 minutes. The zucchini should be tender, the filling heated through, and the cheese melted and lightly browned. Serve.

## Brown Rice And Goat Cheese Croquettes

Servings: 3
Cooking Time: 8 Minutes

**Ingredients:**

- ¾ cup Water
- 6 tablespoons Raw medium-grain brown rice, such as brown Arborio
- ½ cup Shredded carrot
- ¼ cup Walnut pieces
- 3 tablespoons (about 1½ ounces) Soft goat cheese
- 1 tablespoon Pasteurized egg substitute, such as Egg Beaters (gluten-free, if a concern)
- ¼ teaspoon Dried thyme
- ¼ teaspoon Table salt
- ¼ teaspoon Ground black pepper
- Olive oil spray

**Directions:**

1. Combine the water, rice, and carrots in a small saucepan set over medium-high heat. Bring to a boil, stirring occasionally. Cover, reduce the heat to very low, and simmer very slowly for 45 minutes, or until the water has been absorbed and the rice is tender. Set aside, covered, for 10 minutes.
2. Scrape the contents of the saucepan into a food processor. Cool for 10 minutes.
3. Preheat the toaster oven to 400°F.
4. Put the nuts, cheese, egg substitute, thyme, salt, and pepper into the food processor. Cover and pulse to a coarse paste, stopping the machine at least once to scrape down the inside of the canister.
5. Uncover the food processor; scrape down and remove the blade. Using wet, clean hands, form the mixture into two 4-inch-diameter patties for a small batch, three 4-inch-diameter patties for a medium batch, or four 4-inch-diameter patties for a large one. Generously coat both sides of the patties with olive oil spray.
6. Set the patties in the air fryer oven with as much air space between them as possible. Air-fry undisturbed for 8 minutes, or until brown and crisp.
7. Use a nonstick-safe spatula to transfer the croquettes to a wire rack. Cool for 5 minutes before serving.

## Roasted Herbed Shiitake Mushrooms

Servings: 5

Cooking Time: 4 Minutes

**Ingredients:**

- 8 ounces shiitake mushrooms, stems removed and caps roughly chopped
- 1 tablespoon olive oil
- ½ teaspoon salt
- freshly ground black pepper
- 1 teaspoon chopped fresh thyme leaves
- 1 teaspoon chopped fresh oregano
- 1 tablespoon chopped fresh parsley

**Directions:**

1. Preheat the toaster oven to 400°F.
2. Toss the mushrooms with the olive oil, salt, pepper, thyme and oregano. Air-fry for 5 minutes. The mushrooms will still be somewhat chewy with a meaty texture. If you'd like them a little more tender, add a couple of minutes to this cooking time.
3. Once cooked, add the parsley to the mushrooms and toss. Season again to taste and serve.

## Roasted Belgian Endive With Pistachios And Lemon

Servings: 2

Cooking Time: 7 Minutes

**Ingredients:**

- 2 Medium 3-ounce Belgian endive head(s)
- 2 tablespoons Olive oil
- ½ teaspoon Table salt
- ¼ cup Finely chopped unsalted shelled pistachios
- Up to 2 teaspoons Lemon juice

**Directions:**

1. Preheat the toaster oven to 325°F (or 330°F, if that's the closest setting).
2. Trim the Belgian endive head(s), removing the little bit of dried-out stem end but keeping the leaves intact. Quarter the head(s) through the stem (which will hold the leaves intact). Brush the endive quarters with oil, getting it down between the leaves. Sprinkle the quarters with salt.
3. When the machine is at temperature, set the endive quarters cut sides up in the air fryer oven with as much air space between them as possible. They should not touch. Air-fry undisturbed for 7 minutes, or until lightly browned along the edges.
4. Use kitchen tongs to transfer the endive quarters to serving plates or a platter. Sprinkle with the pistachios and lemon juice. Serve warm or at room temperature.

# Sweet Potato Puffs

Servings: 18
Cooking Time: 35 Minutes

**Ingredients:**

- 3 8- to 10-ounce sweet potatoes
- 1 cup Seasoned Italian-style dried bread crumbs
- 3 tablespoons All-purpose flour
- 3 tablespoons Instant mashed potato flakes
- ¾ teaspoon Onion powder
- ¾ teaspoon Table salt
- Olive oil spray

**Directions:**

1. Preheat the toaster oven to 350°F .
2. Prick the sweet potatoes in four or five different places with the tines of a flatware fork (not in a line but all around the sweet potatoes).
3. When the machine is at temperature, set the sweet potatoes in the air fryer oven with as much air space between them as possible. Air-fry undisturbed for 20 minutes.
4. Use kitchen tongs to transfer the sweet potatoes to a wire rack. (They will still be firm; they are only partially cooked.) Cool for 10 to 15 minutes. Meanwhile, increase the machine's temperature to 400°F. Spread the bread crumbs on a dinner plate.
5. Peel the sweet potatoes. Shred them through the large holes of a box grater into a large bowl. Stir in the flour, potato flakes, onion powder, and salt until well combined.
6. Scoop up 2 tablespoons of the sweet potato mixture. Form it into a small puff, a cylinder about like a Tater Tot. Set this cylinder in the bread crumbs. Gently roll it around to coat on all sides, even the ends. Set aside on a cutting board and continue making more puffs: 11 more for a small batch, 17 more for a medium batch, or 23 more for a large batch.
7. Generously coat the puffs with olive oil spray on all sides. Set the puffs in the air fryer oven with as much air space between them as possible. They should not be touching, but even a fraction of an inch will work well. Air-fry undisturbed for 15 minutes, or until lightly browned and crunchy.
8. Gently turn the contents of the air fryer oven out onto a wire rack. Cool the puffs for a couple of minutes before serving.

## Classic Falafel

Servings: 4

Cooking Time: 14 Minutes

**Ingredients:**

- 1 (15-ounce) can low-sodium chickpeas, drained and rinsed
- 3 shallots, roughly chopped
- 3 tablespoons chickpea flour
- ¼ cup fresh parsley, roughly chopped
- 2 tablespoons cilantro, chopped
- 2 teaspoons minced garlic
- 1 teaspoon ground coriander
- 1 teaspoon ground cumin
- ½ teaspoon sea salt
- ⅛ teaspoon allspice
- Oil spray (hand-pumped)

**Directions:**

1. Preheat the toaster oven to 350°F on AIR FRY for 5 minutes.
2. Place the chickpeas in a food processor and pulse until roughly chopped.
3. Add the shallots, flour, parsley, cilantro, garlic, coriander, cumin, salt, and allspice, and pulse to form a thick paste.
4. Roll the chickpea mixture into 2-inch balls and flatten them slightly with the palm of your hand.
5. Place the air-fryer basket in the baking tray and coat it generously with oil spray.
6. Place the falafel in a single layer in the basket. Spray the patties with oil on both sides. You might have to work in batches.
7. Place the tray in position 2 and air fry until golden, turning halfway through, for about 14 minutes in total. Repeat with remaining patties. Serve.

## Balsamic Sweet Potatoes

Servings: 4

Cooking Time: 40 Minutes

**Ingredients:**

- 2 medium sweet potatoes, scrubbed (or peeled) and sliced into 1-inch rounds
- 3 tablespoons olive oil
- 2 tablespoons balsamic vinegar
- 2 teaspoons molasses
- ½ teaspoon garlic powder
- Salt and freshly ground black pepper to taste
- 1 tablespoon grated lemon zest

**Directions:**

1. Preheat the toaster oven to 400° F.
2. Mix the potatoes, oil, balsamic vinegar, molasses, and garlic powder together in an oiled or nonstick 8½ × 8½ × 2-inch square baking (cake) pan. Cover the pan with aluminum foil.
3. BAKE, covered, for 30 minutes, or until tender. Remove the cover.
4. BROIL for 10 minutes, or until the potatoes are lightly browned. Season to taste with salt and pepper and garnish with the lemon zest.

# Salmon Salad With Steamboat Dressing

Servings: 4

Cooking Time: 18 Minutes

**Ingredients:**

- ¼ teaspoon salt
- 1½ teaspoons dried dill weed
- 1 tablespoon fresh lemon juice
- 8 ounces fresh or frozen salmon fillet (skin on)
- 8 cups shredded romaine, Boston, or other leaf lettuce
- 8 spears cooked asparagus, cut in 1-inch pieces
- 8 cherry tomatoes, halved or quartered

**Directions:**

1. Mix the salt and dill weed together. Rub the lemon juice over the salmon on both sides and sprinkle the dill and salt all over. Refrigerate for 15 to 20 minutes.
2. Make Steamboat Dressing and refrigerate while cooking salmon and preparing salad.
3. Cook salmon in air fryer oven at 330°F for 18 minutes. Cooking time will vary depending on thickness of fillets. When done, salmon should flake with fork but still be moist and tender.
4. Remove salmon from air fryer oven and cool slightly. At this point, the skin should slide off easily. Cut salmon into 4 pieces and discard skin.
5. Divide the lettuce among 4 plates. Scatter asparagus spears and tomato pieces evenly over the lettuce, allowing roughly 2 whole spears and 2 whole cherry tomatoes per plate.
6. Top each salad with one portion of the salmon and drizzle with a tablespoon of dressing. Serve with additional dressing to pass at the table.

## Chocolate Caramel Pecan Cupcakes

Servings: 6

Cooking Time: 20 Minutes

**Ingredients:**

- 6 tablespoons all-purpose flour
- 6 tablespoons unsweetened cocoa powder
- ¼ teaspoon baking soda
- ¼ teaspoon baking powder
- ⅛ teaspoon table salt
- 6 tablespoons unsalted butter, softened
- ½ cup granulated sugar
- 1 large egg
- ½ teaspoon pure vanilla extract
- ½ cup sour cream
- BUTTERCREAM FROSTING
- ¼ cup unsalted butter, softened
- 1 ¾ cups confectioners' sugar
- 2 to 3 tablespoons half-and-half or milk
- 1 teaspoon pure vanilla extract
- Caramel ice cream topping
- ¼ cup caramelized chopped pecans

**Directions:**

1. Preheat the toaster oven to 350°F. Line a 6-cup muffin pan with cupcake papers.
2. Whisk the flour, cocoa, baking soda, baking powder, and salt in a small bowl; set aside.
3. Beat the butter and granulated sugar in a large bowl with a handheld mixer at medium-high speed for 2 minutes, or until the mixture is light and creamy. Beat in the egg well. Beat in the vanilla.
4. On low speed, beat in the flour mixture in thirds, alternating with the sour cream, beginning and ending with the flour mixture. The batter will be thick.
5. Spoon the batter evenly into the prepared cupcake cups, filling each about three-quarters full. Bake for 18 to 20 minutes, or until a wooden pick inserted into the center comes out clean. Place on a wire rack and let cool completely.
6. Meanwhile, make the frosting: Beat the butter in a large bowl using a handheld mixer on medium-high speed until creamy. Gradually beat in the confectioners' sugar. Beat in 2 tablespoons of half-and-half and the vanilla. Beat in the remaining tablespoon of half-and-half, as needed, until the frosting is of desired consistency.
7. Frost each cooled cupcake. Drizzle the caramel topping in thin, decorative stripes over the frosting. Top with the caramelized pecans.

# Make-ahead Oatmeal-raisin Cookies

Servings: 8
Cooking Time: 45 Minutes

**Ingredients:**

- 1 cup (5 ounces) all-purpose flour
- ¾ teaspoon table salt
- ½ teaspoon baking soda
- ¼ teaspoon ground cinnamon
- ¾ cup (5¼ ounces) dark brown sugar
- ½ cup (3½ ounces) granulated sugar
- ½ cup vegetable oil
- 4 tablespoons unsalted butter, melted and cooled
- 1 large egg plus 1 large yolk
- 1 teaspoon vanilla extract
- 3 cups (9 ounces) old-fashioned rolled oats
- ½ cup raisins

**Directions:**

1. Adjust toaster oven rack to middle position and preheat the toaster oven to 350 degrees. Line large and small rimmed baking sheets with parchment paper. Whisk flour, salt, baking soda, and cinnamon together in bowl.
2. Whisk brown sugar and granulated sugar together in medium bowl. Whisk in oil and melted butter until combined. Whisk in egg and yolk and vanilla until smooth. Gently stir in flour mixture with rubber spatula until soft dough forms. Fold in oats and raisins until evenly distributed (mixture will be stiff).
3. Working with 3 tablespoons dough at a time, roll into balls. Space desired number of dough balls at least 1½ inches apart on prepared small sheet; space remaining dough balls evenly on prepared large sheet. Using bottom of greased dry measuring cup, press each ball until 2½ inches in diameter.
4. Bake small sheet of cookies until edges are just beginning to brown and centers are still soft but not wet, 10 to 15 minutes. Let cookies cool slightly on sheet. Serve warm or at room temperature.
5. Freeze remaining large sheet of cookies until firm, about 1 hour. Transfer cookies to 1-gallon zipper-lock bag and freeze for up to 1 month. Bake frozen cookies as directed; do not thaw.

# Carrot Cake

Servings: 6
Cooking Time: 30 Minutes

**Ingredients:**

- FOR THE CAKE
- ½ cup canola oil, plus extra for greasing the baking dish
- 1 cup all-purpose flour, plus extra for dusting the baking dish
- 1 cup granulated sugar
- 1 teaspoon baking powder
- ½ teaspoon sea salt
- 2 teaspoons pumpkin pie spice
- 2 large eggs
- 1 cup carrot, finely shredded
- ½ cup dried apricot, chopped
- FOR THE ICING
- 4 ounces cream cheese, room temperature
- ¼ cup salted butter, room temperature
- 1 teaspoon vanilla extract
- 2 cups confectioners' sugar

**Directions:**

1. To make the cake
2. Place the rack in position 1 and preheat the oven to 325°F on BAKE for 5 minutes.
3. Lightly grease an 8-inch-square baking dish with oil and dust with flour.
4. Place the rack in position 1.
5. In a large bowl, stir the flour, sugar, baking powder, salt, and pumpkin pie spice.
6. Make a well in the center and add the oil and eggs, stirring until just combined. Add the carrot and apricot and stir until well mixed.
7. Transfer the batter to the baking dish and bake for about 30 minutes until golden brown and a toothpick inserted in the center comes out clean.
8. Remove the cake from the oven and cool completely in the baking dish.
9. To make the icing
10. When the cake is cool, whisk the cream cheese, butter, and vanilla until very smooth and blended. Add the confectioners' sugar and whisk until creamy and thick, about 2 minutes.
11. Ice the cake and serve.

# Mixed Berry Hand Pies

Servings: 4
Cooking Time: 15 Minutes

**Ingredients:**

- ¾ cup sugar
- ½ teaspoon ground cinnamon
- 1 tablespoon cornstarch
- 1 cup blueberries
- 1 cup blackberries
- 1 cup raspberries, divided
- 1 teaspoon water
- 1 package refrigerated pie dough (or your own homemade pie dough)
- 1 egg, beaten

**Directions:**

1. Combine the sugar, cinnamon, and cornstarch in a small saucepan. Add the blueberries, blackberries, and ½ cup of the raspberries. Toss the berries gently to coat them evenly. Add the teaspoon of water to the saucepan and turn the stovetop on to medium-high heat, stirring occasionally. Once the berries break down, release their juice and start to simmer (about 5 minutes), simmer for another couple of minutes and then transfer the mixture to a bowl, stir in the remaining ½ cup of raspberries and let it cool.
2. Preheat the toaster oven to 370°F.
3. Cut the pie dough into four 5-inch circles and four 6-inch circles.
4. Spread the 6-inch circles on a flat surface. Divide the berry filling between all four circles. Brush the perimeter of the dough circles with a little water. Place the 5-inch circles on top of the filling and press the perimeter of the dough circles together to seal. Roll the edges of the bottom circle up over the top circle to make a crust around the filling. Press a fork around the crust to make decorative indentations and to seal the crust shut. Brush the pies with egg wash and sprinkle a little sugar on top. Poke a small hole in the center of each pie with a paring knife to vent the dough.
5. Air-fry two pies at a time. Brush or spray the air fryer oven with oil and place the pies into the air fryer oven. Air-fry for 9 minutes. Turn the pies over and air-fry for another 6 minutes. Serve warm or at room temperature.

# Peach Cobbler

Servings: 4

Cooking Time: 35 Minutes

**Ingredients:**

- FOR THE FILLING
- 4 cups chopped fresh peaches
- ½ cup sugar
- 2 tablespoons cornstarch
- 1 teaspoon vanilla extract
- FOR THE COBBLER
- 1 cup all-purpose flour
- ¼ cup sugar
- ¾ teaspoon baking powder
- Pinch of sea salt
- 3 tablespoons cold salted butter, cut into ½-inch cubes
- ½ cup buttermilk

**Directions:**

1. To make the filling
2. In a medium bowl, toss together the peaches, sugar, cornstarch, and vanilla.
3. Transfer to an 8-inch-square baking dish. Set aside.
4. To make the cobbler
5. Place the rack in position 1 and preheat the toaster oven to 350°F on BAKE for 5 minutes.
6. In a large bowl, stir the flour, sugar, baking powder, and sea salt.
7. Using your fingertips, rub the butter into the flour mixture until the mixture resembles coarse crumbs.
8. Add the buttermilk in a thin stream to the flour crumbs, tossing with a fork until a sticky dough forms.
9. Scoop the batter by tablespoons and dollop it on the peaches, spacing the mounds out evenly and leaving gaps for the steam to escape.
10. Bake for 35 minutes, or until the cobbler is golden brown and the filling is bubbly.
11. Serve warm.

# Orange Almond Ricotta Cookies

Servings: 24
Cooking Time: 15 Minutes

**Ingredients:**

- Cookie Ingredients
- ½ stick unsalted butter, room temperature
- 1 cup sugar
- 1 large egg
- 1 cup ricotta cheese, drained
- 1½ tablespoons orange juice
- 1 orange, zested
- ¼ teaspoon almond extract
- 1¼ cups all purpose flour
- ½ teaspoon baking powder
- ½ teaspoon salt
- Glaze Ingredients
- 1 cup powdered sugar
- 1½ tablespoons orange juice
- ½ orange, zested

**Directions:**

1. Beat together the butter and sugar for 3 minutes or until light and fluffy.
2. Add the egg, ricotta, orange juice, orange zest, and almond extract and beat until well combined. Add the flour, baking powder, and salt, then fold gently to combine. Don't overmix.
3. Preheat the toaster Oven to 350°F.
4. Line the food tray with parchment paper, then divide the dough into 1½-tablespoon pieces and place on the tray.
5. Insert the tray at mid position in the preheated oven.
6. Select the Bake function, adjust time to 15 minutes, and press Start/Pause.
7. Remove when done and allow cookies to cool completely before glazing.
8. Make the glaze by stirring together the powdered sugar, orange juice, and zest until smooth. According to your preference, add more powdered sugar to make the glaze thicker, or more orange juice to make the glaze thinner.
9. Spoon about ½-teaspoon of the glaze on each cookie and spread gently. Allow the glaze to harden before serving

# Goat Cheese–stuffed Nectarines

Servings: 4

Cooking Time: 10 Minutes

**Ingredients:**

- 4 ripe nectarines, halved and pitted
- 1 tablespoon olive oil
- 1 cup soft goat cheese, room temperature
- 1 tablespoon maple syrup
- ¼ teaspoon vanilla extract
- ¼ teaspoon ground cinnamon
- 2 tablespoons pecans, chopped

**Directions:**

1. Preheat the toaster oven to 350°F on AIR FRY for 5 minutes.
2. Place the air-fryer basket in the baking tray and place the nectarines in the basket, hollow-side up. Brush the tops and hollow of the fruit with the olive oil.
3. In position 2, air fry for 5 minutes to soften and lightly brown the fruit.
4. While the fruit is air frying, in a small bowl, stir the goat cheese, maple syrup, vanilla, and cinnamon until well blended.
5. Take the fruit out and evenly divide the cheese filling between the halves. Air fry for 5 minutes until the filling is heated through and a little melted.
6. Serve topped with pecans.

# Mini Gingerbread Bundt Cakes

Servings: 16

Cooking Time: 24 Minutes

**Ingredients:**

- 3 cups all-purpose flour
- 1/4 cup baking cocoa
- 1 tablespoon baking soda
- 1 teaspoon ground cinnamon
- 1 teaspoon ground ginger
- 1 teaspoon salt
- 1/4 teaspoon ground cloves
- 1/4 teaspoon ground nutmeg
- 1 cup butter, softened
- 1 1/4 cups milk
- 1 cup packed dark brown sugar
- 1 cup molasses
- 2 large eggs
- 1 cup mini chocolate chips Glaze: 1 package (12 oz.) semi-sweet chocolate chips
- 1/3 cup heavy cream
- 2 tablespoons butter
- 2 tablespoons light corn syrup
- Chopped crystallized ginger

**Directions:**

1. Preheat the toaster oven to 350°F. Spray mini bundt pans with nonstick cooking spray. Dust with flour.
2. In a medium bowl, stir together flour, cocoa, baking soda, cinnamon, ginger, salt, cloves and nutmeg.
3. In a large mixer bowl, beat butter until creamy. Gradually beat in milk, brown sugar, molasses and eggs until well blended.
4. Reduce speed to LOW. Slowly add flour mixture until blended. Stir in chocolate chips.
5. Pour into prepared bundt pans.
6. Bake 20 to 24 minutes or until toothpick inserted in center comes out clean.
7. Cool on wire rack 10 minutes. Invert onto cooling rack and cool completely.
8. In a microwavable bowl, stir together 1 cup chocolate chips, heavy cream, butter and corn syrup.
9. Microwave on MEDIUM power 1 minute or until chips are shiny. Stir until mixture is smooth.
10. Spread glaze over top of each mini bundt and sprinkle with crystallized ginger.

# Blueberry Cheesecake Tartlets

Servings: 9

Cooking Time: 6 Minutes

**Ingredients:**

- 8 ounces cream cheese, softened
- ¼ cup sugar
- 1 egg
- ½ teaspoon vanilla extract
- zest of 2 lemons, divided
- 9 mini graham cracker tartlet shells
- 2 cups blueberries
- ½ teaspoon ground cinnamon
- juice of ½ lemon
- ¼ cup apricot preserves

**Directions:**

1. Preheat the toaster oven to 330°F.
2. Combine the cream cheese, sugar, egg, vanilla and the zest of one lemon in a medium bowl and blend until smooth by hand or with an electric hand mixer. Pour the cream cheese mixture into the tartlet shells.
3. Air-fry 3 tartlets at a time at 330°F for 6 minutes, rotating them in the air fryer oven halfway through the cooking time.
4. Combine the blueberries, cinnamon, zest of one lemon and juice of half a lemon in a bowl. Melt the apricot preserves in the microwave or over low heat in a saucepan. Pour the apricot preserves over the blueberries and gently toss to coat.
5. Allow the cheesecakes to cool completely and then top each one with some of the blueberry mixture. Garnish the tartlets with a little sugared lemon peel and refrigerate until you are ready to serve.

## Fried Oreos

Servings: 12
Cooking Time: 7 Minutes

**Ingredients:**

- 1 Large egg white(s)
- 2 tablespoons Water
- 1 cup Graham cracker crumbs
- 12 Original-size Oreos (not minis or king-size)
- Vegetable oil spray

**Directions:**

1. Preheat the toaster oven to 375°F .
2. Set up and fill two shallow soup plates or small pie plates on your counter: one for the egg white(s), whisked with the water until foamy; and one for the graham cracker crumbs.
3. Dip a cookie in the egg white mixture, turning several times to coat well. Let any excess egg white mixture slip back into the rest, then set the cookie in the crumbs. Turn several times to coat evenly, pressing gently. You want an even but not thick crust. However, make sure that the cookie is fully coated and that the filling is sealed inside. Lightly coat the cookie on all sides with vegetable oil spray. Set aside and continue dipping and coating the remaining cookies.
4. Set the coated cookies in the oven with as much air space between them as possible. Air-fry undisturbed for 6 minutes, or until the coating is golden brown and set. If the machine is at 360°F, the cookies may need 1 minute more to cook and set.
5. Use a nonstick-safe spatula to transfer the cookies to a wire rack. Cool for at least 5 minutes before serving.

## Green Grape Meringues

Servings: 4
Cooking Time: 40 Minutes

**Ingredients:**

- 1 cup sugar
- 3 egg whites, beaten until stiff
- ½ teaspoon lemon juice
- Vanilla frozen yogurt
- 1 cup sliced fresh green grapes
- 2 squares unsweetened baking chocolate, shaved
- Nonfat whipped topping

**Directions:**

1. Preheat the toaster oven to 250° F.
2. Add the sugar slowly to the egg white mixture and continue to beat. Add the lemon juice. With a tablespoon, drop on an oiled or nonstick 6½ × 10-inch baking sheet to make a mound of meringue approximately 2 inches across. Make a slight depression in the center of each one.
3. BAKE for 40 minutes, or until crusty and browned. Cool and fill each meringue shell with a scoop of vanilla frozen yogurt. Top with equal portions of green grapes, chocolate shavings, and nonfat whipped topping. The meringues may be stored in an airtight container until ready to use.

# Triple Chocolate Brownies

Servings: 16

Cooking Time: 25 Minutes

**Ingredients:**

- ⅓ cup salted butter, room temperature, plus extra for greasing the baking dish
- ¾ cup brown sugar
- 2 large eggs
- 1 teaspoon vanilla extract
- ½ cup all-purpose flour
- ¼ cup cocoa powder
- ¼ teaspoon baking powder
- ⅛ teaspoon salt
- ½ cup dark chocolate chips
- ¼ cup white chocolate chips

**Directions:**

1. Place the rack in position 1 and preheat the oven to 325°F on BAKE for 5 minutes.
2. Lightly grease a 6-inch-square baking dish with butter.
3. In a large bowl, beat together the butter and sugar with an electric hand beater or a whisk until combined. Add the eggs and vanilla and beat to combine.
4. Beat in the flour, cocoa powder, baking powder, and salt until just combined.
5. Stir in dark chocolate and white chocolate chips, then spoon the batter into the prepared dish.
6. Bake for 25 minutes or until a knife inserted in the center comes out mostly clean.
7. Cool in the baking dish and serve.

## Wild Blueberry Sweet Empanadas

Servings: 12
Cooking Time: 8 Minutes

**Ingredients:**

- 2 cups frozen wild blueberries
- 5 tablespoons chia seeds
- ¼ cup honey
- 1 tablespoon lemon or lime juice
- ¼ cup water
- 1½ cups all-purpose flour
- 1 cup whole-wheat flour
- ½ teaspoon salt
- 1 tablespoon sugar
- ½ cup cold unsalted butter
- 1 egg
- ½ cup plus 2 tablespoons milk, divided
- 1 cup powdered sugar
- 1 teaspoon vanilla extract

**Directions:**

1. To make the wild blueberry chia jam, place the blueberries, chia seeds, honey, lemon or lime juice, and water into a blender and pulse for 2 minutes. Pour the chia jam into a glass jar or bowl and cover. Store in the refrigerator at least 4 to 8 hours or until the jam is thickened.
2. In a food processor, place the all-purpose flour, whole-wheat flour, salt, sugar, and butter and process for 2 minutes, scraping down the sides of the food processor every 30 seconds. Add in the egg and blend for 30 seconds. Using the pulse button, add in ½ cup of the milk 1 tablespoon at a time or until the dough is moist enough to handle and be rolled into a ball. Let the dough rest at room temperature for 30 minutes.
3. On a floured surface, cut the dough in half; then form a ball and cut each ball into 6 equal pieces, totaling 12 equal pieces. Work with one piece at a time, and cover the remaining dough with a towel. Roll out the dough into a 6-inch round, much like a tortilla, with ¼ inch thickness. Place 4 tablespoons of filling in the center of round, fold over to form a half-circle. Using a fork, crimp the edges together and pierce the top with a fork for air holes. Repeat with the remaining dough and filling.
4. Preheat the toaster oven to 350°F.
5. Working in batches, place 3 to 4 empanadas in the air fryer oven and spray with cooking spray. Air-fry for 8 minutes. Repeat in batches, as needed. Allow the sweet empanadas to cool for 15 minutes. Meanwhile, in a small bowl, whisk together the powdered sugar, the remaining 2 tablespoons of milk, and the vanilla extract. Then drizzle the glaze over the surface and serve.

## Little Swedish Coffee Cakes

Servings: 4
Cooking Time: 30 Minutes

**Ingredients:**

- Cake batter:
- 1 cup unbleached flour
- 1 teaspoon baking powder
- ½ cup sugar
- ½ cup finely ground pecans
- ¾ cup low-fat buttermilk
- 1 tablespoon vegetable oil
- 1 egg, lightly beaten
- 1 teaspoon vanilla extract
- Salt to taste
- Sifted confectioners' sugar
- Canola oil for brushing pan

**Directions:**

1. Preheat the toaster oven to 350° F.
2. Combine the cake batter ingredients in a bowl, mixing well. Pour the batter into an oiled or nonstick 8½ × 8½ × 2-inch square baking (cake) pan.
3. BAKE for 30 minutes, or until a toothpick inserted in the center comes out clean. Run a knife around the edge of the pan, invert, and place on a rack to cool. Sprinkle the top with sifted confectioners' sugar and cut into small squares.

## Sour Cream Pound Cake

Servings: 6
Cooking Time: 60 Minutes

**Ingredients:**

- ¾ cup unsalted butter, plus extra for greasing the baking pan
- 2½ cups all-purpose flour, sifted, plus extra for dusting the baking pan
- 1½ cups granulated sugar
- 4 large eggs
- 2 teaspoons pure vanilla extract
- ½ teaspoon baking soda
- ¾ cup sour cream

**Directions:**

1. Place the rack in position 1 and preheat the toaster oven to 350°F on BAKE for 5 minutes.
2. Lightly grease and dust a 9-by-5-inch loaf pan.
3. In a large bowl, cream the butter and sugar with an electric hand beater until very light and fluffy, about 4 minutes.
4. Beat in the eggs one at a time, scraping down the sides of the bowl after each addition.
5. Beat in the vanilla.
6. In a medium bowl, stir the flour and baking soda.
7. Fold the flour mixture and sour cream into the butter mixture, alternating two times each, until well combined.
8. Spoon the batter into the loaf pan and bake for 1 hour, or until a toothpick inserted in the center comes out clean.
9. Let cool completely in the pan and serve.

# Individual Peach Crisps

Servings: 2
Cooking Time: 60 Minutes

**Ingredients:**

- 2 tablespoons granulated sugar, divided
- 1 teaspoon lemon juice
- ¼ teaspoon cornstarch
- ⅛ teaspoon table salt, divided
- 1 pound frozen sliced peaches, thawed
- ⅓ cup whole almonds or pecans, chopped fine
- ¼ cup (1¼ ounces) all-purpose flour
- 2 tablespoons packed light brown sugar
- ⅛ teaspoon ground cinnamon
- Pinch ground nutmeg
- 3 tablespoons unsalted butter, melted and cooled

**Directions:**

1. Adjust toaster oven rack to lowest position and preheat the toaster oven to 425 degrees. Combine 1 tablespoon granulated sugar, lemon juice, cornstarch, and pinch salt in medium bowl. Gently toss peaches with sugar mixture and divide evenly between two 12-ounce ramekins.
2. Combine almonds, flour, brown sugar, cinnamon, nutmeg, remaining pinch salt, and remaining 1 tablespoon granulated sugar in now-empty bowl. Drizzle with melted butter and toss with fork until evenly moistened and mixture forms large chunks with some pea-size pieces throughout. Sprinkle topping evenly over peaches, breaking up any large chunks.
3. Place ramekins on aluminum foil–lined small rimmed baking sheet and bake until filling is bubbling around edges and topping is deep golden brown, 25 to 30 minutes, rotating sheet halfway through baking. Let crisps cool on wire rack for 15 minutes before serving.

# Chocolate Cupcakes With Salted Caramel Buttercream

Servings: 12

Cooking Time: 20 Minutes

**Ingredients:**

- Cake Ingredients
- 1 egg
- ½ cup vegetable oil
- ½ cup buttermilk
- ½ teaspoon vanilla extract
- 1 cup granulated sugar
- 1 cup all-purpose flour
- ¼ cup dark cocoa powder
- 1 teaspoon baking soda
- ½ teaspoon salt
- ½ teaspoon instant espresso powder
- ½ cup boiling water (205°-212°F)
- Buttercream Ingredients
- ½ cup unsalted butter, room temperature
- ⅓ cup caramel sauce, room temperature
- ½ teaspoon vanilla extract
- ½ teaspoon kosher salt
- 1 cup powdered sugar

**Directions:**

1. Whisk together the egg, vegetable oil, buttermilk, and vanilla extract in a bowl and set aside.
2. Sift together sugar, flour, cocoa powder, baking soda, salt, and instant espresso in a large mixing bowl.
3. Add the wet ingredients into the dry and mix until well combined.
4. Pour in the boiling water slowly while whisking vigorously until the batter is smooth.
5. Line the muffin pan with cupcake liners, then pour in the batter.
6. Preheat the toaster Oven to 350°F.
7. Place the cupcakes on the wire rack, then insert the rack at mid position in the preheated oven.
8. Select the Bake and Fan functions, adjust time to 20 minutes, and press Start/Pause.
9. Remove when done and allow cupcakes to cool on a wire rack for 2 hours.
10. Beat butter using a stand mixer on medium speed for 1 minute or until smooth and fluffy.
11. Beat in the caramel sauce, vanilla, and salt for 2 minutes or until well combined. You may need to scrape down the side of the bowl occasionally.
12. Add the powdered sugar slowly, beating on low speed until fully incorporated.
13. Beat the buttercream on medium speed for 2 minutes or until smooth and creamy.
14. Pipe the buttercream onto the cooled cupcake using a decorated tip.
15. Place the cakes in the fridge for 30 minutes before serving.

# Lemon Torte

Servings: 6
Cooking Time: 16 Minutes

**Ingredients:**

- First mixture:
- ¼ cup margarine, at room temperature
- ½ teaspoon grated lemon zest
- 3 egg yolks
- ¼ cup sugar
- ⅓ cup unbleached flour
- 3 tablespoons cornstarch
- Second mixture:
- 3 egg whites
- 2 tablespoons sugar
- Cream Cheese Frosting (recipe follows)

**Directions:**

1. Beat together the first mixture ingredients in a medium bowl with an electric mixer until the mixture is smooth. Set aside. Clean the electric mixer beaters.
2. Beat the second mixture together: Beat the egg whites into soft peaks in a medium bowl, gradually adding the sugar, and continue beating until the peaks are stiff. Fold the first mixture into the second mixture to make the torte batter.
3. Pour ½ cup torte batter into a small oiled or nonstick 3½ × 7½ × 2¼-inch loaf pan.
4. BROIL for 1 or 2 minutes, or until lightly browned. Remove from the oven.
5. Pour and spread evenly another ½ cup batter on top of the first layer. Broil again for 1 or 2 minutes, or until lightly browned. Repeat the process until all the batter is used up. When cool, run a knife around the sides to loosen and invert onto a plate. Chill. Frost with Cream Cheese Frosting and serve chilled.

# Freezer-to-oven Chocolate Chip Cookies

Servings: 6
Cooking Time: 15 Minutes

**Ingredients:**

- 2 ½ cups all-purpose flour
- 1 teaspoon baking soda
- ½ teaspoon table salt
- ¼ teaspoon baking powder
- 1 cup unsalted butter, softened
- 1 cup packed dark brown sugar
- ¾ cup granulated sugar
- 2 large eggs
- 2 teaspoons pure vanilla extract
- 1 (12-ounce) package semisweet chocolate chips

**Directions:**

1. Preheat the toaster oven to 375°F. Line a 12 x 12-inch baking sheet with parchment paper.
2. Whisk the flour, baking soda, salt, and baking powder in a medium bowl; set aside.
3. Beat the butter, brown sugar, and granulated sugar in a large bowl with a handheld mixer at medium-high speed for 2 minutes or until creamy. Beat in the eggs, one at a time, beating well after each addition. Beat in the vanilla. Mix in the dry ingredients until blended. Stir in the chocolate chips.
4. Using a 2-tablespoon scoop, shape the batter into balls about 1 ½ inches in diameter. Arrange the cookies 1 inch apart on the prepared baking sheet. Bake for 13 to 15 minutes or until golden brown. Remove from the oven and let cool for 1 minute, then transfer the cookies to a wire rack.

# POULTRY

## Jerk Chicken Drumsticks

Servings: 2
Cooking Time: 20 Minutes

**Ingredients:**

- 1 or 2 cloves garlic
- 1 inch of fresh ginger
- 2 serrano peppers, (with seeds if you like it spicy, seeds removed for less heat)
- 1 teaspoon ground allspice
- 1 teaspoon ground nutmeg
- 1 teaspoon chili powder
- ½ teaspoon dried thyme
- ½ teaspoon ground cinnamon
- ½ teaspoon paprika
- 1 tablespoon brown sugar
- 1 teaspoon soy sauce
- 2 tablespoons vegetable oil
- 6 skinless chicken drumsticks

**Directions:**

1. Combine all the ingredients except the chicken in a small chopper or blender and blend to a paste. Make slashes into the meat of the chicken drumsticks and rub the spice blend all over the chicken (a pair of plastic gloves makes this really easy). Transfer the rubbed chicken to a non-reactive covered container and let the chicken marinate for at least 30 minutes or overnight in the refrigerator.
2. Preheat the toaster oven to 400°F.
3. Transfer the drumsticks to the air fryer oven. Air-fry for 10 minutes. Turn the drumsticks over and air-fry for another 10 minutes. Serve warm with some rice and vegetables or a green salad.

# Honey Lemon Thyme Glazed Cornish Hen

Servings: 2
Cooking Time: 20 Minutes

**Ingredients:**

- 1 (2-pound) Cornish game hen, split in half
- olive oil
- salt and freshly ground black pepper
- ¼ teaspoon dried thyme
- ¼ cup honey
- 1 tablespoon lemon zest
- juice of 1 lemon
- 1½ teaspoons chopped fresh thyme leaves
- ½ teaspoon soy sauce
- freshly ground black pepper

**Directions:**

1. Split the game hen in half by cutting down each side of the backbone and then cutting through the breast. Brush or spray both halves of the game hen with the olive oil and then season with the salt, pepper and dried thyme.
2. Preheat the toaster oven to 390°F.
3. Place the game hen, skin side down, into the air fryer oven and air-fry for 5 minutes. Turn the hen halves over and air-fry for 10 minutes.
4. While the hen is cooking, combine the honey, lemon zest and juice, fresh thyme, soy sauce and pepper in a small bowl.
5. When the air fryer oven timer rings, brush the honey glaze onto the game hen and continue to air-fry for another 3 to 5 minutes, just until the hen is nicely glazed, browned and has an internal temperature of 165°F.
6. Let the hen rest for 5 minutes and serve warm.

# Philly Chicken Cheesesteak Stromboli

Servings: 2

Cooking Time: 28 Minutes

**Ingredients:**

- ½ onion, sliced
- 1 teaspoon vegetable oil
- 2 boneless, skinless chicken breasts, partially frozen and sliced very thin on the bias (about 1 pound)
- 1 tablespoon Worcestershire sauce
- salt and freshly ground black pepper
- ½ recipe of Blue Jean Chef pizza dough, or 14 ounces of store-bought pizza dough
- 1½ cups grated Cheddar cheese
- ½ cup Cheese Whiz® (or other jarred cheese sauce), warmed gently in the microwave
- tomato ketchup for serving

**Directions:**

1. Preheat the toaster oven to 400°F.
2. Toss the sliced onion with oil and air-fry for 8 minutes, stirring halfway through the cooking time. Add the sliced chicken and Worcestershire sauce to the air fryer oven, and toss to evenly distribute the ingredients. Season the mixture with salt and freshly ground black pepper and air-fry for 8 minutes, stirring a couple of times during the cooking process. Remove the chicken and onion from the air fryer oven and let the mixture cool a little.
3. On a lightly floured surface, roll or press the pizza dough out into a 13-inch by 11-inch rectangle, with the long side closest to you. Sprinkle half of the Cheddar cheese over the dough leaving an empty 1-inch border from the edge farthest away from you. Top the cheese with the chicken and onion mixture, spreading it out evenly. Drizzle the cheese sauce over the meat and sprinkle the remaining Cheddar cheese on top.
4. Start rolling the stromboli away from you and toward the empty border. Make sure the filling stays tightly tucked inside the roll. Finally, tuck the ends of the dough in and pinch the seam shut. Place the seam side down and shape the Stromboli into a U-shape to fit in the air-fry oven. Cut 4 small slits with the tip of a sharp knife evenly in the top of the dough and lightly brush the stromboli with a little oil.
5. Preheat the toaster oven to 370°F.
6. Spray or brush the air fryer oven with oil and transfer the U-shaped stromboli to the air fryer oven. Air-fry for 12 minutes, turning the stromboli over halfway through the cooking time. (Use a plate to invert the stromboli out of the air fryer oven and then slide it back into the air fryer oven off the plate.)
7. To remove, carefully flip stromboli over onto a cutting board. Let it rest for a couple of minutes before serving. Slice the stromboli into 3-inch pieces and serve with ketchup for dipping, if desired.

## Chicken Hand Pies

Servings: 8
Cooking Time: 10 Minutes

**Ingredients:**

- ¾ cup chicken broth
- ¾ cup frozen mixed peas and carrots
- 1 cup cooked chicken, chopped
- 1 tablespoon cornstarch
- 1 tablespoon milk
- salt and pepper
- 1 8-count can organic flaky biscuits
- oil for misting or cooking spray

**Directions:**

1. In a medium saucepan, bring chicken broth to a boil. Stir in the frozen peas and carrots and air-fry for 5 minutes over medium heat. Stir in chicken.
2. Mix the cornstarch into the milk until it dissolves. Stir it into the simmering chicken broth mixture and cook just until thickened.
3. Remove from heat, add salt and pepper to taste, and let cool slightly.
4. Lay biscuits out on wax paper. Peel each biscuit apart in the middle to make 2 rounds so you have 16 rounds total. Using your hands or a rolling pin, flatten each biscuit round slightly to make it larger and thinner.
5. Divide chicken filling among 8 of the biscuit rounds. Place remaining biscuit rounds on top and press edges all around. Use the tines of a fork to crimp biscuit edges and make sure they are sealed well.
6. Spray both sides lightly with oil or cooking spray.
7. Cook in a single layer, 4 at a time, at 330°F for 10 minutes or until biscuit dough is cooked through and golden brown.

# Fried Chicken

Servings: 4
Cooking Time: 40 Minutes

**Ingredients:**

- 12 skin-on chicken drumsticks
- 1 cup buttermilk
- 1½ cups all-purpose flour
- 1 tablespoon smoked paprika
- ¾ teaspoon celery salt
- ¾ teaspoon dried mustard
- ½ teaspoon garlic powder
- ½ teaspoon freshly ground black pepper
- ½ teaspoon sea salt
- ½ teaspoon dried thyme
- ¼ teaspoon dried oregano
- 4 large eggs
- Oil spray (hand-pumped)

**Directions:**

1. Place the chicken and buttermilk in a medium bowl, cover, and refrigerate for at least 1 hour, up to overnight.
2. Preheat the toaster oven to 375°F on AIR FRY for 5 minutes.
3. In a large bowl, stir the flour, paprika, celery salt, mustard, garlic powder, pepper, salt, thyme, and oregano until well mixed.
4. Beat the eggs until frothy in a medium bowl and set them beside the flour.
5. Place the air-fryer basket in the baking tray and generously spray it with the oil.
6. Dredge a chicken drumstick in the flour, then the eggs, and then in the flour again, thickly coating it, and place the drumstick in the basket. Repeat with 5 more drumsticks and spray them all lightly with the oil on all sides.
7. In position 2, air fry for 20 minutes, turning halfway through, until golden brown and crispy with an internal temperature of 165°F.
8. Repeat with the remaining chicken, covering the cooked chicken loosely with foil to keep it warm. Serve.

# Buffalo Egg Rolls

Servings: 8
Cooking Time: 9 Minutes

**Ingredients:**

- 1 teaspoon water
- 1 tablespoon cornstarch
- 1 egg
- 2½ cups cooked chicken, diced or shredded (see opposite page)
- ⅓ cup chopped green onion
- ⅓ cup diced celery
- ⅓ cup buffalo wing sauce
- 8 egg roll wraps
- oil for misting or cooking spray
- Blue Cheese Dip
- 3 ounces cream cheese, softened
- ⅓ cup blue cheese, crumbled
- 1 teaspoon Worcestershire sauce
- ¼ teaspoon garlic powder
- ¼ cup buttermilk (or sour cream)

**Directions:**

1. Mix water and cornstarch in a small bowl until dissolved. Add egg, beat well, and set aside.
2. In a medium size bowl, mix together chicken, green onion, celery, and buffalo wing sauce.
3. Divide chicken mixture evenly among 8 egg roll wraps, spooning ½ inch from one edge.
4. Moisten all edges of each wrap with beaten egg wash.
5. Fold the short ends over filling, then roll up tightly and press to seal edges.
6. Brush outside of wraps with egg wash, then spritz with oil or cooking spray.
7. Place 4 egg rolls in air fryer oven.
8. Air-fry at 390°F for 9 minutes or until outside is brown and crispy.
9. While the rolls are cooking, prepare the Blue Cheese Dip. With a fork, mash together cream cheese and blue cheese.
10. Stir in remaining ingredients.
11. Dip should be just thick enough to slightly cling to egg rolls. If too thick, stir in buttermilk or milk 1 tablespoon at a time until you reach the desired consistency.
12. Cook remaining 4 egg rolls as in steps 7 and 8.
13. Serve while hot with Blue Cheese Dip, more buffalo wing sauce, or both.

# Chicken Cordon Bleu

Servings: 4

Cooking Time: 25 Minutes

**Ingredients:**

- Oil spray (hand-pumped)
- 4 (4-ounce) chicken breasts
- 4 teaspoons Dijon mustard
- 4 slices Gruyère cheese
- 4 slices lean ham
- 1 cup all-purpose flour
- 2 large eggs
- 1 cup bread crumbs
- ½ cup Parmesan cheese

**Directions:**

1. Preheat the toaster oven to 350°F on AIR FRY for 5 minutes.
2. Place the air-fryer basket in the baking tray and generously spray it with the oil.
3. Place a chicken breast flat on a clean work surface and cut along the length of the breast, almost in half, holding the knife parallel to the counter. Open the breast up like a book and place it between two pieces of plastic wrap. Pound the chicken breast to about ¼-inch thick with a rolling pin or mallet. Repeat with the remaining breasts.
4. Spread the mustard on each breast, place a piece of cheese and ham in the center, and fold the sides of the breast over the cheese and ham. Roll the breast up from the unfolded sides to form a sealed packet. Secure with a toothpick.
5. Repeat with the remaining breasts.
6. Sprinkle the flour on a plate and set it on your work surface.
7. In a small bowl, whisk the eggs until well beaten and place next to the flour.
8. In a medium bowl, stir the bread crumbs and Parmesan and place next to the eggs.
9. Dredge the chicken rolls in the flour, then egg, then the bread crumb mixture, making sure they are completely breaded.
10. Arrange the chicken in the basket and spray lightly all over with the oil.
11. In position 2, air fry for 25 minutes, turning halfway through, until golden brown. Serve.

## Chicken Chunks

Servings: 4
Cooking Time: 10 Minutes

**Ingredients:**

- 1 pound chicken tenders cut in large chunks, about 1½ inches
- salt and pepper
- ½ cup cornstarch
- 2 eggs, beaten
- 1 cup panko breadcrumbs
- oil for misting or cooking spray

**Directions:**

1. Season chicken chunks to your liking with salt and pepper.
2. Dip chicken chunks in cornstarch. Then dip in egg and shake off excess. Then roll in panko crumbs to coat well.
3. Spray all sides of chicken chunks with oil or cooking spray.
4. Place chicken in air fryer oven in single layer and air-fry at 390°F for 5 minutes. Spray with oil, turn chunks over, and spray other side.
5. Air-fry for an additional 5 minutes or until chicken juices run clear and outside is golden brown.
6. Repeat steps 4 and 5 to cook remaining chicken.

# Parmesan Crusted Chicken Cordon Bleu

Servings: 2
Cooking Time: 14 Minutes

**Ingredients:**

- 2 (6-ounce) boneless, skinless chicken breasts
- salt and freshly ground black pepper
- 1 tablespoon Dijon mustard
- 4 slices Swiss cheese
- 4 slices deli-sliced ham
- ¼ cup all-purpose flour
- 1 egg, beaten
- ¾ cup panko breadcrumbs
- ⅓ cup grated Parmesan cheese
- olive oil, in a spray bottle

**Directions:**

1. Butterfly the chicken breasts. Place the chicken breast on a cutting board and press down on the breast with the palm of your hand. Slice into the long side of the chicken breast, parallel to the cutting board, but not all the way through to the other side. Open the chicken breast like a "book". Place a piece of plastic wrap over the chicken breast and gently pound it with a meat mallet to make it evenly thick.
2. Season the chicken with salt and pepper. Spread the Dijon mustard on the inside of each chicken breast. Layer one slice of cheese on top of the mustard, then top with the 2 slices of ham and the other slice of cheese.
3. Starting with the long edge of the chicken breast, roll the chicken up to the other side. Secure it shut with 1 or 2 toothpicks.
4. Preheat the toaster oven to 350°F.
5. Set up a dredging station with three shallow dishes. Place the flour in the first dish. Place the beaten egg in the second shallow dish. Combine the panko breadcrumbs and Parmesan cheese together in the third shallow dish. Dip the stuffed and rolled chicken breasts in the flour, then the beaten egg and then roll in the breadcrumb-cheese mixture to cover on all sides. Press the crumbs onto the chicken breasts with your hands to make sure they are well adhered. Spray the chicken breasts with olive oil and transfer to the air fryer oven.
6. Air-fry at 350°F for 14 minutes, flipping the breasts over halfway through the cooking time. Let the chicken rest for a few minutes before removing the toothpicks, slicing and serving.

# Chicken Schnitzel Dogs

Servings: 4

Cooking Time: 10 Minutes

**Ingredients:**

- ½ cup flour
- ½ teaspoon salt
- 1 teaspoon marjoram
- 1 teaspoon dried parsley flakes
- ½ teaspoon thyme
- 1 egg
- 1 teaspoon lemon juice
- 1 teaspoon water
- 1 cup breadcrumbs
- 4 chicken tenders, pounded thin
- oil for misting or cooking spray
- 4 whole-grain hotdog buns
- 4 slices Gouda cheese
- 1 small Granny Smith apple, thinly sliced
- ½ cup shredded Napa cabbage
- coleslaw dressing

**Directions:**

1. In a shallow dish, mix together the flour, salt, marjoram, parsley, and thyme.
2. In another shallow dish, beat together egg, lemon juice, and water.
3. Place breadcrumbs in a third shallow dish.
4. Cut each of the flattened chicken tenders in half lengthwise.
5. Dip flattened chicken strips in flour mixture, then egg wash. Let excess egg drip off and roll in breadcrumbs. Spray both sides with oil or cooking spray.
6. Air-fry at 390°F for 5 minutes. Spray with oil, turn over, and spray other side.
7. Air-fry for 3 to 5 minutes more, until well done and crispy brown.
8. To serve, place 2 schnitzel strips on bottom of each hot dog bun. Top with cheese, sliced apple, and cabbage. Drizzle with coleslaw dressing and top with other half of bun.

# Lemon Chicken

Servings: 4
Cooking Time: 36 Minutes

**Ingredients:**

- Marinade:
- Juice of 1 lemon, plus pulp (no seeds)
- ¼ cup dry white wine
- 2 tablespoons olive oil
- 1 tablespoon minced garlic
- 2 bay leaves
- 1 teaspoon dried thyme
- 1 teaspoon freshly ground black pepper
- Salt to taste
- 8 skinless, boneless chicken thighs
- Juice of 1 lemon
- 2 tablespoons olive oil

**Directions:**

1. Preheat the toaster oven to 400° F.
2. Blend the marinade ingredients in a bowl (reserving 3 tablespoons for basting), add the chicken thighs, cover, and chill for at least 1 hour. Transfer the chicken thighs to a 1-quart 8½ × 8½ × 4-inch ovenproof baking dish. Adjust the seasonings. Cover the dish with aluminum foil.
3. BAKE for 30 minutes, or until the chicken is tender. Uncover and spoon the reserved marinade over the chicken.
4. BROIL for 8 minutes, or until lightly browned. Remove the bay leaves before serving.

# Chicken-fried Steak With Gravy

Servings: 2

Cooking Time: 16 Minutes

**Ingredients:**

- FOR THE STEAK
- Oil spray (hand-pumped)
- 1 cup all-purpose flour
- 1 teaspoon garlic powder
- 1 teaspoon onion powder
- 1 teaspoon smoked paprika
- 2 large eggs
- 2 (½-pound) cube steaks
- Sea salt, for seasoning
- Freshly ground black pepper, for seasoning
- FOR THE GRAVY
- 2 tablespoons salted butter
- 2 tablespoons all-purpose flour
- 1½ cups whole milk
- ¼ cup heavy (whipping) cream
- Sea salt, for seasoning
- Freshly ground black pepper, for seasoning

**Directions:**

1. To make the steak
2. Preheat the toaster oven to 400°F on AIR FRY for 5 minutes.
3. Place the air-fryer basket in the baking tray and spray it generously with the oil.
4. In a medium bowl, stir the flour, garlic powder, onion powder, and paprika until well blended.
5. In a medium bowl, beat the eggs and place them next to the flour.
6. Season the steaks all over with salt and pepper.
7. Dredge a steak in the egg and then in the flour mixture, making sure it is well coated. Shake off any excess flour.
8. Place the steak in the basket and repeat the process with the other steak.
9. Spray the tops of the steaks with the oil.
10. In position 2, air fry for 9 minutes until golden brown and crispy. Turn the steaks over, spray the second side with the oil, and air fry for an additional 7 minutes.
11. Set the steaks aside to rest for 5 minutes.
12. To make the gravy
13. While the steak is air frying, melt the butter in a medium saucepan over medium-high heat.
14. Whisk in the flour and cook for 2 minutes until lightly browned.
15. Whisk in the milk until the gravy is creamy and thick, about 5 minutes. Whisk in the cream and season with salt and pepper.
16. Serve the steak topped with the gravy.

# Thai Chicken Drumsticks

Servings: 4
Cooking Time: 20 Minutes

**Ingredients:**

- 2 tablespoons soy sauce
- ¼ cup rice wine vinegar
- 2 tablespoons chili garlic sauce
- 2 tablespoons sesame oil
- 1 teaspoon minced fresh ginger
- 2 teaspoons sugar
- ½ teaspoon ground coriander
- juice of 1 lime
- 8 chicken drumsticks (about 2½ pounds)
- ¼ cup chopped peanuts
- chopped fresh cilantro
- lime wedges

**Directions:**

1. Combine the soy sauce, rice wine vinegar, chili sauce, sesame oil, ginger, sugar, coriander and lime juice in a large bowl and mix together. Add the chicken drumsticks and marinate for 30 minutes.
2. Preheat the toaster oven to 370°F.
3. Place the chicken in the air fryer oven. It's ok if the ends of the drumsticks overlap a little. Spoon half of the marinade over the chicken, and reserve the other half.
4. Air-fry for 10 minutes. Turn the chicken over and pour the rest of the marinade over the chicken. Air-fry for an additional 10 minutes.
5. Transfer the chicken to a plate to rest and cool to an edible temperature. Pour the marinade from the bottom of the air fryer oven into a small saucepan and bring it to a simmer over medium-high heat. Simmer the liquid for 2 minutes so that it thickens enough to coat the back of a spoon.
6. Transfer the chicken to a serving platter, pour the sauce over the chicken and sprinkle the chopped peanuts on top. Garnish with chopped cilantro and lime wedges.

## Italian Baked Chicken

Servings: 4
Cooking Time: 28 Minutes

**Ingredients:**

- 1 pound boneless, skinless chicken breasts
- ½ cup dry white wine
- 3 tablespoons olive oil
- 2 tablespoons white wine vinegar
- 2 tablespoons fresh lemon juice
- 2 teaspoons Italian seasoning
- 3 cloves garlic, minced
- ½ teaspoon kosher salt
- ¼ teaspoon freshly ground black pepper
- 4 slices salami, cut in half
- 3 tablespoons shredded Parmesan cheese

**Directions:**

1. If the chicken breasts are large and thick, slice each breast in half lengthwise. Place the chicken in a shallow baking dish.
2. Combine the white wine, olive oil, vinegar, lemon juice, Italian seasoning, garlic, salt, and pepper in a small bowl. Pour over the chicken breasts. Cover and refrigerate for 2 to 8 hours, turning the chicken occasionally to coat.
3. Preheat the toaster oven to 375 °F.
4. Drain the chicken, discarding the marinade, and place the chicken in an ungreased 12 x 12-inch baking pan. Bake, uncovered, for 20 to 25 minutes or until the chicken is done and a meat thermometer registers 165 °F. Place one slice salami (two pieces) on top of each piece of the chicken. Sprinkle the Parmesan evenly over the chicken breasts and broil for 2 to 3 minutes, or until the cheese is melted and starting to brown.

## Orange-glazed Roast Chicken

Servings: 6
Cooking Time: 100 Minutes

**Ingredients:**

- 1 3-pound whole chicken, rinsed and patted dry with paper towels
- Brushing mixture:
- 2 tablespoons orange juice concentrate
- 1 tablespoon soy sauce
- 1 tablespoon toasted sesame oil
- 1 teaspoon ground ginger
- Salt and freshly ground black pepper to taste

**Directions:**

1. Preheat the toaster oven to 400° F.
2. Place the chicken, breast side up, in an oiled or nonstick 8½ × 8½ × 2-inch square (cake) pan and brush with the mixture, which has been combined in a small bowl, reserving the remaining mixture. Cover with aluminum foil.
3. BAKE for 1 hour and 20 minutes. Uncover and brush the chicken with remaining mixture.
4. BAKE, uncovered, for 20 minutes, or until the breast is tender when pierced with a fork and golden brown.

# Apricot Glazed Chicken Thighs

Servings: 2

Cooking Time: 22 Minutes

**Ingredients:**

- 4 bone-in chicken thighs (about 2 pounds)
- olive oil
- 1 teaspoon salt
- ¼ teaspoon freshly ground black pepper
- ½ teaspoon onion powder
- ¾ cup apricot preserves 1½ tablespoons Dijon mustard
- ½ teaspoon dried thyme
- 1 teaspoon soy sauce
- fresh thyme leaves, for garnish

**Directions:**

1. Preheat the toaster oven to 380°F.
2. Brush or spray both the air fryer oven and the chicken with the olive oil. Combine the salt, pepper and onion powder and season both sides of the chicken with the spice mixture.
3. Place the seasoned chicken thighs, skin side down in the air fryer oven. Air-fry for 10 minutes.
4. While chicken is cooking, make the glaze by combining the apricot preserves, Dijon mustard, thyme and soy sauce in a small bowl.
5. When the time is up on the air fryer oven, spoon half of the apricot glaze over the chicken thighs and air-fry for 2 minutes. Then flip the chicken thighs over so that the skin side is facing up and air-fry for an additional 8 minutes. Finally, spoon and spread the rest of the glaze evenly over the chicken thighs and air-fry for a final 2 minutes. Transfer the chicken to a serving platter and sprinkle the fresh thyme leaves on top.

## Sweet-and-sour Chicken

Servings: 6

Cooking Time: 10 Minutes

**Ingredients:**

- 1 cup pineapple juice
- 1 cup plus 3 tablespoons cornstarch, divided
- ¼ cup sugar
- ¼ cup ketchup
- ¼ cup apple cider vinegar
- 2 tablespoons soy sauce or tamari
- 1 teaspoon garlic powder, divided
- ¼ cup flour
- 1 tablespoon sesame seeds
- ½ teaspoon salt
- ¼ teaspoon ground black pepper
- 2 large eggs
- 2 pounds chicken breasts, cut into 1-inch cubes
- 1 red bell pepper, cut into 1-inch pieces
- 1 carrot, sliced into ¼-inch-thick rounds

**Directions:**

1. In a medium saucepan, whisk together the pineapple juice, 3 tablespoons of the cornstarch, the sugar, the ketchup, the apple cider vinegar, the soy sauce or tamari, and ½ teaspoon of the garlic powder. Cook over medium-low heat, whisking occasionally as the sauce thickens, about 6 minutes. Stir and set aside while preparing the chicken.
2. Preheat the toaster oven to 370°F.
3. In a medium bowl, place the remaining 1 cup of cornstarch, the flour, the sesame seeds, the salt, the remaining ½ teaspoon of garlic powder, and the pepper.
4. In a second medium bowl, whisk the eggs.
5. Working in batches, place the cubed chicken in the cornstarch mixture to lightly coat; then dip it into the egg mixture, and return it to the cornstarch mixture. Shake off the excess and place the coated chicken in the air fryer oven. Spray with cooking spray and air-fry for 5 minutes, and spray with more cooking spray. Cook an additional 3 to 5 minutes, or until completely cooked and golden brown.
6. On the last batch of chicken, add the bell pepper and carrot to the air fryer oven and cook with the chicken.
7. Place the cooked chicken and vegetables into a serving bowl and toss with the sweet-and-sour sauce to serve.

Printed by Libri Plureos GmbH in Hamburg,
Germany